THE WOLF CYCLE

ROBERT BAUTNER
LARA HELMLING

Library of Congress Control Number: 2025909721
Paperback ISBN: 979-8-9887884-6-1
First edition

Printed in the United States of America. Orders by U.S. trade bookstores and wholesalers. Manufactured and printed in the United States of America.

Publisher: Integrity Publishing International
Houston, Texas, United States

Email: *Team@IntegrityPub.com*
www.IntegrityPublishingInternational.com

DEDICATION

To God the Eternal Father, his son, Jesus, and their cohort, the Holy Ghost. Particularly, I am grateful for God watching over me and blessing me with the protection of what humans call autism.

–Robert

To my son Lliam, thank you for

always believing in me

–Lara

CONTENTS

PRAISE FOR THE WOLF CYCLE

The three little pigs story just got markedly better through the observant eyes and inquisitive mind of Robert Bautner. Surprisingly insightful and delightfully revealing, his retelling of the story will have you seeing yourself in one of the three gifted and creative little porkers and finding ways to stave off the big bad wolves in your life. Deeper and more meaningful than you ever thought a seemingly juvenile tale could be, it will affect you more than you might want to admit. Read *The Wolf Cycle* and watch your own life get undeniably better as you come to understand yourself more clearly.

Dale S., Salt Lake City, UT

Prior to reading this book, I was not well-versed in personality types, nor had I understood fully how my personality type affects (or can affect) my true nature either in positive or negative ways. For this reason, I found *The Wolf Cycle* compelling, as it explained personality types in a way that was understandable and effective for me. (Full review at the end of the book)

Stan S., Salt Lake City, UT

The Wolf Cycle is easy to read and apply the principles. Robert is insightful and vulnerable, and he shares how we can identify where we are in *The Wolf Cycle* and how to overcome the wolf within.

Jessica C., Salt Lake City, UT

I have been fortunate enough to read *The Wolf Cycle,* which is one of the best books I have read. It is very relatable to my life experience, and I would like to share a few of my thoughts with you. We all fall into the category of personalities mentioned, which is the straw, stick, and brick. We need to know who we are, figure out our strengths and weaknesses, and seek to work on ourselves. This will enable us to build a well-structured and strong house so that the wolves, both in the world and in us, will not eat us up and destroy us. (Full review at the end of the book)

Bampoe A., Ghana

I met Robert when he was 19. He was just coming out of a rough childhood where his mother was very hard on him. His autistic mind was such a challenge for her. Nothing she said or did worked. Robert's brilliant mind makes this book fascinating to read. He has overcome much and now inspires all of us.

Richard C., Salt Lake City, UT

The examples that are given are very vivid and help the reader to really see inside each of the characters and view the world through their eyes. I truly enjoyed reading and then rereading this book to try to understand which pig I really am, and I know you will enjoy it as well. (Full review at the end of the book)

Adam W., Salt Lake City, UT

The Wolf Cycle is amazing! If you are looking to learn about humanity and what it takes to communicate and connect with individuals on a core level, look no further. This book is brilliantly written to teach us that every human on this planet is different in their own special way. We need to learn how to connect in a deeper way to make this world go around in such a beautiful way.

Speaker Erik Swanson, Award-Winning Motivational Speaker

ACKNOWLEDGEMENTS

To all of the people whose ears I bent in developing this theory...

To all those who unwittingly played a role as I observed them participate in the wolf cycle, as innocents or as wolves…

To those who discussed with me their ideas of personality and human life, who played their own part in inspiring me to form this theory…

To my children and my friends who always support me in my writing, even when they think I'm a little cuckoo…

To my editor and co-author Lara Helmling, who understood my riddles and translated them into this book…

To my autism therapist, Dr. Julia Connelly, whose faint suggestion that I write a book has become a major passion in my life…

To Erik Swanson and Jon Kovach Jr. for helping me get this book in published form…

Most of all, I want to thank God my Father, Jesus my Savior, and the Holy Spirit, for the inspiration, love, and protection they give me every day…

–Robert

To my son Lliam and my dear friends Kevyn, Melissa, Alice, and Sandy: thank you for encouraging me and standing by me through thick and thin.

To Dr. Parrish, thank you for your insight and wisdom.

To Stephen, thank you for being part of my life for so many years.

To Robert, whose innocent and unique perspective on the world made this book possible.

To God, whose love I am still coming to understand, thank you for choosing me.

–Lara

FOREWORD

In his newest book *The Wolf Cycle,* Robert Bautner has created a fresh window into human psychology and social interactions with practical insights, personal experiences and observations, and helpful self-awareness tips to perceive and extricate oneself from the key affront that has constantly existed in the human experiences: the mortal enmity in the form of a wolf at the door.

Robert shares deep and personally-witnessed evidences of the wolf and its role as a weapon against the mainspring of human progress, the very one which impedes human development in societal interactions, self-growth, social and institutional influences, creativity and innovation.

It is ripened timing to prime human consciousness for the full potential and realization of what is greatest in the divine course of humanity. Robert details the many ways in which our divine innocence is clouded by ignorance, fear and prejudice, thus hampering and distracting people from expressing into the world beauty, harmony, elevation, and mighty wonders of art and ingenuity.

Robert's pointed and insightful exposé will enable the reader to become more aware, more conscientious, and more proactive in recognizing, avoiding, and disempowering the wolves of destruction while allowing each of us to express our divine purpose creatively according to the blueprint which lies within us. We do not deny our nature; rather, we acknowledge our divinity and influence the world with decreasing self-impediments as we become aware of and amplify ourselves against the pallid and counterproductive destroyers of what will empower each of us to live most authentically in our innocence and become destroyers of ignorance in the evolving golden age.

Richard R. Bowman, MA (Linguistics, Near Eastern Studies, Secondary Education)

INTRODUCTION

We all know the story of the three little pigs. Three pigs, each with a different house, each attacked by a wolf, and only one withstands the blows: the brick building pig. In the first published version of 1886, the stick and straw-building pigs are eaten by the wolf and only the brick pig survives.

Yet this is not the original story. It actually traces its origins far earlier in oral history. In the first recorded English fairytale, it is not three pigs and a wolf but three pixies and a fox. Pixies, in Celtic folklore, were small, trickster spirits who inhabited the woods. They would spook horses, steal shiny objects, and otherwise make a nuisance of themselves. In some communities, pixies were thought to be the spirits of unbaptized children who had died. Over time, pixies became pigsies, which then became pigs. In all of the stories, the creatures have built houses out of different materials, and only the one with the strongest house survives. As we heard the story in modern day, we understood that we did not want our house blown down by the wolf, so we naturally concluded that we should want a brick house.

It is worth noting that the first published version of *The Three Little Pigs* was in 1886 by author James Halliwell-Phillipps. Halliwell's edition, with which we are most familiar, featured the survival of the pig in the brick house and the unfortunate demise of the stick and straw building pigs. His ending seems to indicate that the brick house is superior, but I believe if we disregard that element of his version and look at the personalities of the three pigs, his story identifies personality secrets as well as the roots of good and evil in the human psyche.

So…

What if we look at the story through a different lens?

What if we see each attack and its results as a learning exercise? What if we looked at the failures of the stick and straw homes as an opportunity to learn how to use sticks or straw better in building a house…instead of deciding sticks and straw should not be used at all?

It is true that brick will withstand the most attacks right from the start, but they fail to give the builder flexibility in the ebb and flow of life. Sticks and straw have more 'give' that enable the builder to achieve different goals than bricks.

All of this is to say that each building material has its strengths and weaknesses. Each has its gifts and talents, if you will.

In the version that you are about to read, I have considered how the three pigs and their building materials might point to archetypes in the human experience. I have pondered how the pigs' behaviors might have contributed to their future. This led me to consider how human behavior contributes to future outcomes. Taking these ideas and then observing them over time, I have found that they do indeed describe three core personality types. All of us clearly and distinctly fall into one of the three categories. We all, in our authenticity, behave as a stick, straw, or brick builder. Importantly, I have also observed that none of us vacillate between types. We are all solidly one of the three types. I have found no exceptions.

With this in mind, I have rewritten and expanded on the original story of the three pigs and the wolf. I have considered the progeny of the three little pigs and what might have happened in later generations. In my version, the mama pig and her triplets live years after their brick-building ancestor, and they have all been taught to build only out of brick so that they might survive the wolf. Just prior to where our story picks up, disaster has struck the family. Papa and Mama pig had built a home as they had been taught, out of brick. But Papa, Mama's one true love, was a visionary who felt restricted by the hardness and coldness of bricks. Mama, pregnant with the triplets at the time, was not certain, but she believed in him. He felt sure they could build their house out of sticks and be both safe and free to live fully and happily. Tragically, as Papa was putting the finishing touches on his beautiful stick dream home, the wolf came knocking. Papa's house fell, and Papa was eaten by the wolf.

History has proven time and time again; those who fail to learn from the past, experience both its grace or its pain. In this case a stick builder, Papa Pig, collided with the wolf, and because of misinformation and a neglect of the lessons of the past, he built with inferior forms of his material. This ended in pain for the family, as a legacy of misinformation was passed on. The damage was done. The only positive way forward for the family's progenitors was to turn the negative outcome into a positive result for future generations.

It was critical they do this without malice towards the wolf. If they were to enter into the blame game, they would see themselves as the victim and never analyze their strategy and develop better methods. Then, any research would be in vain, and the same poor results would once again repeat themselves, and the experiences would have been lost to history. In the course of it all, they would lose an invaluable historical understanding that could have enabled future generations to avoid repeating the experience over again.

Mama was left to birth and raise the triplets on her own. She grieved for the loss of her beloved, and the loss of his dream. She became determined to preserve his memory in how she raised the triplets. His singular idea was that sticks could be used to build a safe and happy home, if one so desired. Mama still believed in his dream, but now she wondered, how? She went to work, researching the stick as a building material. She realized that the home must be made of bigger sticks! Using logs or lumber was the key. Once the home was made of lumber, it would be just as strong as the brick house. This got her thinking. What if the straw, too, could be a strong home? Again, she began to read, research, and explore ideas. Triumphantly, she concluded that yes, it was possible. If one used the right kind of straw and used packed bales or woven rope instead of loose straw, the home would be strong.

She set out to teach her children to build a strong home, but she knew that if the homes were to be truly theirs, they needed to discover the best building methods on their own. As they grew into young adults, she guided them to make good choices based in freedom, deviating from her family history yet doing so with better information and, she prayed, better results.

The day came to begin their instruction. The first thing they had to know was how their father died. They had to understand that their choices would determine their future and even their survival for generations to come. She sat them down. She told them the truth. They were devastated, to say the least. Bob, who had already begun dreaming of building a stick home, cried piteously. Mama consoled them all, encouraging them to understand that there was no bad material; there were only poor building methods.

Throughout the family's history, they had resided in the authenticity of their true nature. That authenticity is what I (Robert) call divine innocence (we will explore this concept of divine innocence in depth as we go along). One might think that this should have been enough to protect them, but it was not. It was not until Mama did the research that the family was able to stay true to their innocence and simultaneously avoid an untimely demise at the hands of the wolf. Without this research, history would no doubt have repeated itself. I emphasize this now, because in my observations a lack of critical thinking and research into how one is living and how one constructs one's life can be extremely costly. Even in innocence, we can lack the information we need to protect ourselves, our families, and our freedom. When this happens, we fail to experience life fully. This was the case of Papa Pig. He knew that having a brick home was outside of his innocence, but he did not have the information he needed to build a strong stick home. Mama set out to change that.

What the Three Little Pigs and the Big Bad Wolf Teach Us About Ourselves

Many of us also live the way we are told simply because a parent or caregiver taught us to do so, or because society says we need to do so in order to survive. This can push us out of our personality type, creating confusion, restlessness, or even depression. Sometimes, it tragically results in our becoming the wolf. To get back to who we truly are, secure in our divine innocence, we must first be able to identify which type of builder we are, learn about our type, and then protect our divine innocence at all costs.

The first step, then, is to question the conclusion that the pigs chose in the original story: that the brick material was the only viable building option. The building materials were the fall guy, which points more to the mental laziness of the builders than any factual basis for the brick's superiority. In reality, the mental aspect was the real culprit.

The original pigs did no research, no planning as to how to build a strong home of their favored material, and thus they failed. When one does not apply understanding along with discernment, history repeats itself to create an unfortunate ending once again. Because Papa's life was sacred to Mama, the wolf unintentionally drove her to figure out how to guide her children to build safety into their decisions. A better result would come about not by being lazy but by being diligent to understand what caused their father's death.

The family habit of brick building had arisen because the brick builder's home survived the wolf's attack, and he lived to tell the tale. It was his innocence that inspired him to build out of brick. His innocence naturally gave him the upper hand to defeat the wolf and live.

Throughout this story, we see the home as a symbol of our souls, the essence of our lives. Viewing it through this lens, the lesson we must learn is that building our lives requires action to prevent and protect our souls and the lives of those around us from danger. But it is not enough to be authentic. It is not enough to reside in our divine innocence. In reality it was the innocence of the straw and stick pigs that cost them their lives. By ignoring the wolves in the world, they built lives that were too weak to withstand danger. This is true of our lives, too. A world without the wolf of destruction does not exist. When it happens, it feels inconceivable, but we have seen it too often to ignore the fact that there are times when the good will die young, when the innocent–without action, knowledge, or understanding–will perish.

The truth is that the wolf exists in each of us as well as in the world. We each have the capacity to destroy and hate, just as we have the ability to create and love. Divine innocence in its pure form connects to the purity of our souls and is driven by love and creativity. Yet when that innocence mingles with the influences of the wolf within or becomes loosed into our souls, it can lead to confusion, disarray, and ignorance. This confusion can lead to the demise of our innocence. Sadly, human nature often leads us to choose the wolf over innocence, perhaps out of familiarity, perhaps out of fear or the perception of the wolf's power. Yet that 'power' is pure illusion. In fact, the glitz and glamor of the wolf is based in a misunderstanding of what is true and real. It is ignorance. For this reason, throughout this book, we refer to the wolf and its ways as ignorance of truth. The wolf builds nothing of his own. Sometimes he destroys others' work, and other times he claims others' work as his own. In either case, he only takes. He consumes. He does not give, and he does not produce. He is neither a builder nor a creator.

What if someone has chosen to be the wolf? Can they return to innocence? Or are they sentenced to ignorance for the rest of their lives? Underlying this is the central issue of whether we have the choice to be the innocent pig or the ignorant wolf. Initially, we might think yes, of course the wolf can choose to give up his ignorance and become innocent again. Yet there is a problem. Ignorance, by definition, means that one does not know something very important. In this case, the wolf does not know that he is the wolf. He is ignorant of the fact that he is ignorant.

Thus, the wolf has choices. He has agency and can change. But will he? That depends on whether he can become aware of something that is invisible to him. This is why we call innocence divine. Whatever one thinks of one's higher power, of God, a central tenet of this book is that we have a Creator and we need our Creator to know the truth about ourselves, one another, and creation. It is only through connection with the divine that we are able to access our innocence, which is the essence of our divinity. Until then, we remain hopelessly ignorant.

The first step to accepting God's influence, to give up the wolf in our souls, is to embrace the humility to be wrong, that we cannot figure out the truth on our own. The gift of humility is not found in mortality, nor is it buried in the earth. It is not found in our intellect nor even in the wisdom of age. Humility is found deep in the senses of the soul. Innocence in itself cannot progress without humility.

The second step, after humbling oneself before the Divine, is to seek the truth, acknowledging that the truth may not be what one expects. This requires us to embrace three gifts. First, there is the gift of challenge. That is, we must challenge the status quo within ourselves. Second, there is the gift of discernment. We can only discern the truth with God's help. We must understand that we cannot rely solely on our own limited reasoning. Finally, there is the gift of confirmation. We must be ready to accept confirmation from the Spirit of that truth that is revealed to us.

While some may have these gifts naturally, we believe there are those who have gone through such horrendous experiences in life, that these gifts are awakened only after surviving the wolf one or more times. Sometimes it is when we are broken, even shattered, that we allow these gifts into our souls. Not all have to go through such experiences, but some do. It is only after the survival of such destruction that they experience the gift of innocence in its full value. Trauma, then, may awaken our innocence, enabling us to discern a lie that is being perpetrated on us. It is awakened when we realize in humility that we cannot change what is happening, and perhaps we cannot withstand the pain of it. This is when ignorance begins to awaken as innocence.

Yet trauma can also further solidify the wolf in the person's soul if they view the trauma as further evidence for the lies they believe. A lie is the wolf of destruction. It is ignorance. What is the one thing that enables people to move from ignorance to innocence? A single thought rooted in humility.

The main emphasis of this book will be on the innocent builders, the three pigs and their personality styles. You will see yourself in one of them, we assure you. We encourage you to explore your divine innocence, yet we also would like you to take note of where your innocence might be faltering due to the wolves of the world, or even the wolf within you.

The Three Pigs and their Building Styles

In my observations, the different building materials of the three little pigs correlate perfectly with the three personality types that we see in people. We call these types the stick, the straw, and the brick, based on the story of The Three Little Pigs. But what is a personality in the first place? What does it mean to say that these are personality types? In my view, a personality is the combination of behaviors, perceptions, and thought patterns. It is how we interpret things that people say and how we respond to experiences. A personality, then, is the expression of our unique self, our divine nature, our divine innocence.

These personalities serve individual purposes in society. Each personality contributes unique gifts to the world and finds joy in different types of work. Together, they form a perfect trifecta of human activity, one that maximizes business success, family life, and personal development. When they collaborate, they create a mosaic of productivity, creativity, and fulfillment.

Human behavior is ideally rooted in these innate personalities, though many people find themselves trying to fit into a different type than what they really are–just like the stick- and straw-building pigs who join the brick-building pig in her house instead of rebuilding their own on better principles. When we turn away from our own type, we deny our truth. We deny what we will call in this book our 'divine innocence.' We have all done this at one time or another.

We also deny our divine innocence when we compete or when we try to force others to be like us or to give us what we want. When we do this, we become the wolf. This is what we call living in ignorance. Each of us is equally capable of living in our divine innocence as a pig or in our ignorance as a wolf.

When we choose to live in our divine innocence as a stick, brick, or straw pig, we build a safe and loving home. This home is our soul, and we find our security within its walls. Our souls are created by God, so to live in divine innocence means to stay true to how God made us no matter what. If we are attacked by a wolf, we always have the power to stay strong in our divine innocence, but we don't always recognize that strength.

If we succumb to the wolf outside our door, we experience fear, hatred, or anger, and we move from innocence to ignorance. Our divinely innocent personality, our divine way of expressing ourselves, is always within us, but when we become the wolf we become ignorant of that innocence. We feel driven out of our home. This leads us to attack others or ourselves, because we feel homeless and so we go in search of someone else's home to inhabit. We seek to regain control and have a home once again. If we do not attack others, we might attack ourselves through negative self-talk, self-sabotage, or worse, self-harm. When we do this, we begin desiccating our own home even more, exacerbating the destruction that the wolf initiated. Sometimes the internal forces that compel us to attack others or ourselves are beyond our perception and our ability to describe them, particularly when they are deeply ingrained into us from childhood.

Builder Personality Comparison Chart			
Builder Type	Core Traits	Blind Spots	Famous Examples
Stick	Freedom-minded, charismatic, takes center stage	Selfish, overconfident, rude	Princess Diana, Clint Eastwood
Brick	Community builder, visionary, grounded, powerful	Rigid, resistant to change, overbearing	Margaret Thatcher, Frank Lloyd Wright
Straw	Deep intellectual insight, connector, helper, playful	Impatient with incompetence, authority driven, lazy	Stephen Hawking, Socrates

So the goal is to build our homes in the strength and power of our divine innocence. With a strong home, the wolf will not be able to blow our houses down. Thus, we will be able to stay in our homes even when the wolf comes huffing and puffing. This is true whether our homes are made of sticks, bricks, or straw.

This brings me to the most important question of this book:

Which house would you build?

The answer to this question will come to you as you read further. Additionally, you will develop the ability to see these types in others, understanding people better by knowing whether they are the stick, straw, or brick personality. You will learn to stand in your divine innocence so that you do not succumb to the idea that another builder type is better than you. You will also learn how to recognize and withstand the attacks of any wolf that comes to your door, no matter what builder type they are.

The One Thing

I would ask one thing of you as you read: be curious.

This is an entirely new way of looking at personality that we are offering you today, and whenever we encounter something brand new we tend to reject it because we cannot connect it easily with what we already know.

Curiosity enables us to discover new horizons because we are willing to take in information that is so new, so different from what we have seen before, that it expands our minds and our lives.

When I (Robert) first observed this expansion in myself, after working with these ideas for some time, I noticed that my relationships began to improve. I found that I was able to observe others' personalities and behaviors in such a way that I better appreciated them for who they are. I was able to work with them more effectively.

I experienced a new sense of peace and confidence in myself, because I was accepting who I was more firmly than ever before.

Perhaps now is a good time to mention the reason for my unique perspective and the source of my authority in these matters. It is not from an institution or even from society. It is a God-given *in*ability to live outside my divine innocence. I am unable to abandon my soul, my home in this world. I am autistic. I do not have a degree in psychology or in the study of personality or of autism or anything else. Nevertheless, I hold the diagnosis of autism. In my view, this is much more powerful and insightful for the purposes of this book than any educational degree.

I received my diagnosis from the University of Utah. I strive to use this diagnosis to help you. It is to help you understand some of the discoveries I have made because of the nature of my autistic mind. Who I am (and am not) within my autistic mind is normal to me. I see things and understand things in a way that more neurotypical people might say is unique. I see algorithms in personalities, patterns of behavior in people, and I see it all through the lens of divine innocence.

When I wrote my memoir *Stop Your Crying*, I had no idea that I had gone through awful traumas until I finished writing the last chapter. I thought my mother was just an anomaly growing up, because I had accepted her abusive behavior as normal. I was dumbfounded, even in a state of shock, when I learned to view her treatment of me from a healthy perspective. I wanted to weep, but I could not find a single tear in me. At first I could not figure out why I could not see the abuses, even though I was 55 years old and 'should have known.' Through further discussions with trusted friends and advisors, and through my own growing understanding of my unique approach to life, I discovered that at the root of it all was the fact that I had never lost that state of divine innocence into which we are all born.

While the non-autistic go to college to teach the autistic how to be non-autistic, my desire is to teach the non-autistic how to appreciate the autistic and learn from us. To appreciate autism for its gift of perspective and its special access to divine innocence is to accept aspects of divine innocence that would otherwise remain hidden.

The Birth of a Grounded Theory of Personality

I developed this theory of personality through hundreds of observations. Whenever I meet someone, I immediately begin to observe their behavior. I look for signs of their personality such as what language they use, how they dress, and what they are interested in. I have even spent time observing the actions and characteristics of historical figures. My tendency is to seek for and recognize patterns in human behavior. I have been told this is a characteristic of having an autistic mind.

I realized that the observations I make are all clues to their personality type. From this qualitative research and from discussions with other authorities in the field, I discovered three personality types. As I reflected on these three types, I realized that they correlated with the three little pigs and their building materials: sticks, straw, and bricks. These many observations are the reason that I am confident that the theory in this book is more than a nice idea: it is a scientific theory. It is what Brené Brown calls a grounded scientific theory. I believe this is an excellent way to describe this work. As I publish this book, I pray that people like you, dear reader, will test it for yourself and contribute more to the evidence for it–or against it.

But how can I call this theory 'scientific?' Science is about observing the world, forming a hypothesis to explain what you see, testing that hypothesis, and adjusting if needed. This is the purest form of science, the kind that does not merely test pre-existing hypotheses. It forms a new hypothesis from observed data and tests it qualitatively. From this process, a theory is born. That's exactly what I did. One rule of science is to stay fair and open-minded, not letting your hopes or opinions cloud what you find. For me, being autistic helps with this. While some autistic people prefer to be alone, I have always been curious about how people behave. My mind naturally stays neutral, which allows me to see things clearly and fairly.

Over time, I have tested my ideas on the people I meet, famous figures in history, and even on myself. I realized that by understanding our personalities—the stick, straw, or brick builders—we can better understand the people around us. Even more importantly, we can learn how to protect ourselves from the wolves in life. Wolves are those who bring destruction, chaos, and harm. They don't build; they destroy. By staying true to your innocence and learning how to work with people of different strengths, you can stand strong and achieve things you couldn't do alone.

This book is about more than personalities; it is my contribution to save civilization from the wolves in the world (and in ourselves). As you discover the three builder types you will come to understand why people do what they do, learning why the three pigs built their homes the way they did. In doing so you will find new insights into relating to others, bringing peace and fulfillment into your life (and theirs) in greater ways. This is the key to keeping the wolves at bay, especially the wolf within your own soul.

Together, we can build a world where the wolf doesn't win.

How The Three Little Pigs Can Save the World

By unlocking the algorithms that lie within the allegory of *The Three Little Pigs*, I have hope that we can more effectively pursue our individual dreams, follow our personal desires and expand our God-given talents. By living within the freedom of our divine innocence, we expand the good in this world. We do not need to confront the hostilities of evil in our world, including those who form secret alliances bent on destroying humanity, because our divine innocence, collectively exercised in our individual lives, is more powerful than any evil. Why? Because evil is always ignorance. It is always weak and powerless…unless we give it our power.

Those of us who stand strong in our divine innocence are the ones with power. We are the ones who create, who build, who have shelter and goodness for ourselves and our families. We build beautiful homes. On the other hand, the wolf has no home. He creates nothing but illusions of power and hate. Martin Luther King Junior said this beautifully when he wrote, "Darkness cannot drive out darkness. Only light can do that. Hate cannot drive out hate. Only love can do that."

We must stand strong in the houses we build, whichever building type we are gifted with, and never let in the wolf at the door. We must resist the urge to engage with wolves who propagate or support cataclysmic efforts to depopulate, dehumanize or bring war to our door steps. Their hopes of wiping out the advancement of civilization or encouraging dissent, including murdering, sterilization and other forms of personal infringements, will fail as long as we stand strong.

And so I ask you, dear reader, to read this book in an effort to answer my original question: 'Which house would you build?'

If you have spent a lifetime denying your divine innocence, you may have to work a little harder to find the answer to that question. In that case, the first question to answer is, 'which house was gifted to you?' This second question must be asked when the wolf has caused destruction to your home and you no longer feel at home in your own soul. In the aftermath of that destruction, you must ask yourself, 'How will I build a better house knowing what I know now?'

CHAPTER 1

THE RETURN TO INNOCENCE

Divine innocence is the only authentic and real state of being. Innocence protects the mind while radiating a godly aura. Divine innocence compels us to live with our eye on the present moment as each one unfolds before us. Our very existence in that moment of time is impactful beyond anything we can comprehend. It is allowing your divine innocence to express itself in its fullness without comparing oneself to others.

How to Identify Divine Innocence

Innocence fills the soul. The depth of real happiness, true knowledge, confidence, and faith comes from the core of our divine innocence.

If we find ourselves unhappy over extended periods of time, it is worth looking inward. This unhappiness may stem from a disconnection from our divine innocence. Without this connection, our souls can falter, and many ill effects may follow. The further we stray from our innocence, the less meaningful life can appear.

However, it is important to recognize that divine innocence does not guarantee constant happiness. There are real and natural moments in life—like the loss of a loved one—that bring sorrow. In these moments, grief, though heavy, is not a sign of being disconnected from innocence. On the contrary, grief is an expression of love and a sacred burden of our humanity.

Divine innocence cannot be purchased, traded, bartered, or manipulated. It must be recognized within and practiced. While innocence often leads to happiness, this happiness is not the result of perfect circumstances. Instead, it comes from the choice to find peace and strength in the midst of life's challenges. To be divinely innocent is not to ignore sadness but to allow space for it when appropriate, trusting that happiness will eventually return.

We often hear people say, "You deserve to be happy." But the word 'deserve' feels misplaced when speaking from the perspective of innocence. Instead, the language of innocence reminds us, "You can choose to seek happiness where it is possible." When happiness is elusive, we should ask ourselves why. Is it because we are under attack by a wolf? If so, our task is to identify the wolf and determine whether it can be confronted or if our innocence requires us to bear the burden. For example, if the wolf is grief from the death of a loved one, our divine innocence calls us to grieve fully and honestly. Grief is not happiness, but it is not a sign of failure; it is an authentic and innocent response to loss.

Unlocking the Power of Divine Innocence

When we discover our divine innocence, we become empowered. It transforms our lives from ignorance and weakness to strength. The story of *The Wizard of Oz* shows us this perfectly. The tin man searches for a heart that feels, the cowardly lion goes on a brave search for courage, and the scarecrow seeks an intelligent brain that calculates. Each of them had these gifts within them all along. It was not the wizard that granted them the attributes they searched for; it was the arduous journey that revealed the truth.

"When we don't understand our innocence, let alone the divinity of others, the wolf in us fills the void with ignorance."

We do not want it to be this way. We want our gifts handed to us on a silver platter. Yet the truth of the matter is that it is the conflicts we face, it is the strain and stress of the battles we fight, that lead us to strength. These problems are the only way we will ever learn to build a house that can stand in divine innocence, strong against the attacks of the wolf.

If we dig a bit deeper into our three friends from *The Wizard of Oz,* we see that their individual dreams are indicative of the unique expressions of their divine innocence. Each of them represents one of the three archetypes of personality that we will explore in this book, but more on that later.

Taking this even further, Dorothy's search for a way home ends in a way that is similar to the lion, scarecrow, and tin man in that she had the gift she was looking for all along. She had the power to go home. Truly, she never left home. She dreamed the whole thing. Her difficult journey away from the truth of who she was only happened in the dark recesses of her imagination. The journey, the wizard, and even her companions do not give her strength or even knowledge. Her ability to go home, to be home, is within her. Her home, in this analogy, is her divine innocence. When she leaves home or believes she is not at home, she is living in ignorance. As we will learn, when someone moves into a state of ignorance they have become the wolf.

Too often, we find ourselves in an endless cycle of searching. We chase motivational quotes, catchy phrases, and the wisdom of inspirational books, hoping they will help us create positive attitudes within ourselves and those around us. We attend motivational seminars and rallies, convinced they hold the key to unlocking our greatness. When those efforts fall short, we turn to mentors, inspiring organizations, or personal coaches, believing they will guide us toward achieving our dreams and fulfilling our potential.

We seek a full bank account, personal fulfillment, meaningful relationships, and peace within our souls. Yet, despite countless hours, money spent, and energy exhausted, we find ourselves confused and frustrated when those aspirations remain out of reach. At some point in our search, we should ask ourselves a crucial question: Have we sought to understand, embrace, or give credence to our inner truth—to our divine innocence?

For most of us, the answer is no. And yet, our divine innocence is the key that unlocks everything we are searching for. When we reconnect with this core part of ourselves and choose to live in it, we gain access to a treasure trove of abilities, insights, and strengths we never realized we had. It is within our divine innocence that true happiness, unshakable faith, and profound knowledge reside.

The good news is that the end of our journey is also its beginning. Like Dorothy in *The Wizard of Oz*, we never truly left home. Our divine innocence has always been within us, though we may have wandered far in the dark recesses of our minds. The harder truth is that reclaiming and living in our divine innocence requires a fundamental shift. It demands a new mindset and habits. We must retrain our thoughts, make different choices, and even recondition our bodies to produce new physiological responses. This is no small task, but it is the pathway to the peace, fulfillment, and strength we have been seeking all along.

If you find yourself tempted to dismiss this idea with a casual 'whatever,' it might be time to search a little deeper within yourself. Denying the truth of our divine innocence often stems from being blind to it for a long time. But once we start to recognize it, something remarkable happens—we gain the power to make meaningful changes in our lives. This recognition is just the beginning. To live in divine innocence, we must also learn to make innocent decisions.

Embracing Innocent Decisions

At first glance, you might assume that making innocent decisions involves being gullible, naïve, or uninformed. In reality, the opposite is true. Innocent decisions are grounded in strength, truth, and integrity—

"Innocent decisions are grounded in strength, truth, and integrity—the defining traits of divine innocence."

the defining traits of divine innocence. Unlike the fragility of secular innocence, divine innocence provides clarity and wisdom to navigate life's challenges. We will explore these distinctions further as we go along, but for now, recognize that divine innocence empowers us to see clearly and act wisely.

To embrace innocent decisions, we must be mindful of what we allow into our five conscious senses. This attentiveness is as important as making deliberate choices in critical areas like career, relationships, and finances. The TV shows we watch, the music we listen to, the scents we absorb, and most importantly, the words we speak—all shape our inner world and our connection to divine innocence. While this list could extend endlessly, the true task is for you to reflect on how these choices affect your life.

If we were to give you all the answers, they would belong to me, not you. The real power comes when you take the time to identify and own your solutions. When you do, the rewards are immense: greater strength in your relationships, deeper peace of mind, and a renewed sense of clarity on your personal journey toward fulfillment and solace.

The five physical senses we learn about in grade school—sight, hearing, taste, touch, and smell—are just the beginning. Our perception extends far beyond these. Some of these "forgotten senses" are closely tied to our divine innocence. Empaths, for instance, use extraordinary senses to perceive invisible realities through deep, soul-level feelings. These emotions, while physical in some ways, serve as a gateway to connecting with the world on a deeper level. Unlike everyday feelings that react to external stimuli, these soul-level perceptions carry unique significance and wisdom.

Other overlooked senses include our perception of time, balance, pain, direction, and even an inner awareness of what is happening within our bodies. For many, these senses have been dulled by the veils we construct to shield ourselves from the world. Yet these subtle senses, honest and unfiltered, whisper directly to our souls. They often emerge in fleeting moments, like the brief brilliance of a shooting star. If we do not capture them in writing or some other tangible way, these revelations vanish just as quickly, leaving us wondering, "What did I just think or feel?"

When we are with others, we may earnestly ask, "Can you repeat that?" in an effort to preserve and fully grasp the message. These insights, born from our inner senses, arise from the purest source—our divine innocence. Sadly, they are fleeting unless we pause to explore and embrace their meaning. Preserving these moments is a vital step on the journey of innocence, offering opportunities for profound transformation.

Reflecting on and capturing these brilliant flashes of insight can illuminate our souls in extraordinary ways. They bring clarity, truth, and the pure light of God into our lives. In such moments, we experience the essence of enlightenment, hearing the true word within ourselves. It is in these instances that we are truly at home in our souls.

Divine Innocence Exposes the Truth

Divine innocence is like a built-in radar that helps us identify what is true and what is not. It acts as our personal truth detector, raising a red flag when something false enters our awareness—whether it comes from a casual comment, a TV statement, or an article we read. When we are in tune with our divine innocence, we instinctively know if something resonates as true or false. This instinct often reveals itself as a gut feeling or an intuitive sense in our other perceptions. In this way, divine innocence highlights truth and exposes lies. When we live in alignment with our divine innocence, we become builders of good— whether we are stick, brick, or straw builders—each contributing uniquely to the fabric of creation.

Divine Innocence vs. Ignorance Comparison

Aspect	Divine Innocence	Ignorance
Perspective	Clarity & Curiosity	Distorted & Defensive
Emotion	Peace & Compassion	Anger & Fear
Motivation	Love & Creation	Control & Destruction
Response to Conflict	Understanding & Forgiveness	Blame & Retaliation
Behavioral Outcome	Builds, Creates, Heals	Destroys, Consumes, Manipulates

However, when we succumb to cowardice or take the easy way out, we betray our divine innocence. Rejecting what we know is right allows the wolf within us to take over. That wolf represents ignorance. It can appear as misleading information, deceitful people, or even everyday frustrations like an irate motorist. When the wolf takes control, it drives us to dominate, manipulate, or reject others. Why? Because we have abandoned the truth of our souls—our home—and feel adrift. In our search for a sense of belonging, we lash out, hoping to gain stability by invading someone else's "home."

For builders living in divine innocence, the ignorance of others—their wolf nature—can be deeply frustrating. Builders are skilled and diligent, naturally inclined to excel in their talents and abilities. They are not misled by fleeting theories or ideologies. When they encounter ignorance, builders may roll their eyes or feel impatient. Yet, they must guard against letting this frustration turn into pride or superiority. Pride is its own form of ignorance. Remembering the phrase "they don't know what they don't know" can help innocent builders maintain understanding and compassion while staying grounded in their own truth.

The wolf, for their part, often dismisses challenges to their ignorance. To others, their lack of awareness may be obvious early on in a conversation or relationship, but it takes a builder operating in divine innocence to see this ignorance for what it truly is. To escape their wolf-like state, individuals must reconnect with their divine innocence. That is where they find protection from the wolf within and around them. It is also where they rediscover their true "home," perfectly designed for who they are. This is their divine soul, their dream home.

Fair warning: ignoring our divine innocence leads to surrendering our souls—our true homes. Sadly, many of us have unknowingly given up our divine innocence to external influences: societal pressures, institutions, media, or even family dynamics. In doing so, we let the wolves of others drive us to abandon our homes and, in turn, become wolves ourselves. This pattern is evident in groupthink phenomena like riots, cancel culture, or road rage. By reclaiming our divine innocence, we can resist these forces. We can return to the sanctuary of our souls, finding peace in our hearts, minds, and spirits—a peace that no wolf can shake.

The Incarceration of the Soul

If we asked you, "Who are the most vulnerable in our society?" who would you choose? Babies? Young children? The elderly? The mentally challenged? The incarcerated? Most people would choose babies. Babies are not only secularly innocent; they are also divinely innocent. Their divine innocence makes them profoundly influential. When they cry, people feel compelled to help. When they coo, they bring smiles and joy. Babies are cared for around the clock, drawing others to them as they radiate divine innocence.

But who are the most vulnerable in society when it comes to divine innocence? It is those whose innocence is most at risk of being overrun by the wolf within—those most susceptible to ignorance and destruction. Wolves never build; they only destroy. If you chose the incarcerated, you would be correct. Those who are incarcerated are confined with limited resources and surrounded by wolves they cannot escape. Their challenge is immense: to resist the wolf within themselves and remain connected to their divine innocence. Though difficult, it is not impossible. With focused hearts and minds, even the most vulnerable can reclaim their divine innocence, but the obstacles they face are substantial.

Claiming our divine innocence is critical for everyone, whether society views us as "normal" or not. Those with autism, ADHD, bipolar disorder, or other sensory or cognitive differences are often labeled as "disordered," but they have a core divine innocence that must not be ignored. As an autistic person, I (Robert) understand this innately. For autistic individuals, this divine innocence is intrinsic and undeniable, but for "normal" people, it can feel as though there is a price to pay for their normalcy. Society often demands that they sacrifice their divine innocence in order to fit in.

The truth is that our institutions—schools, governments, corporations—can be deeply wolfish. They push us to abandon our divine innocence in exchange for societal success, forcing us to conform to their definitions of normalcy. Many accept this bargain, but others resist, often becoming entrepreneurs or small business owners to protect their divine innocence. It is possible to succeed without sacrificing one's soul, but it takes greater effort, particularly when navigating the expectations of institutional systems.

This widespread abandonment of innocence is why we began this chapter by saying, "The innocent feels for the souls of the innocent." We grieve for those who have surrendered their innocence under societal pressures. We see the mistakes we make when we betray our true selves for conformity or, worse, when we impose our demands and expectations on others, forcing them to betray their own innocence for our convenience.

Institutions define normalcy and label deviations as "disorders," "diseases," or "conditions" that require fixing—or worse, as conditions beyond repair. Such labels often isolate people, cutting them off from the rest of society. Medications are prescribed to enforce conformity. Unique perspectives, such as those of autistic or ADHD individuals, are dismissed as deficiencies rather than celebrated as divine gifts. Emotional sensitivities like anxiety and depression, which connect people empathetically to God and others, are treated as illnesses rather than cherished as reflections of profound connection.

Too often, we are told we must choose between being "normal" or "not." The underlying message is that normalcy is the only acceptable goal. This wolfish perspective ignores the beauty and freedom found in divine innocence. To accept such a worldview is to deny the central role divine innocence should play in our lives. Embracing divine innocence allows us to live authentically, rejecting the ignorance of societal conformity and reclaiming the strength, truth, and beauty within our souls.

The Continuum of Thinking Outside the Box

A continuum represents a range from one extreme to another. When we consider "thinking outside the box," we must also consider the mental boxes we live in—those shaped by the world around us. For example, we live in a society that was imagined and built by others. Someone else designed the transportation systems we use, created the clothes we wear, and constructed the houses we live in. Even as you read this book, you are engaging with my thoughts and allowing them into your mind. These external influences shape who we think we are, forming the mental boxes that frame our thoughts and actions.

Thinking "inside the box" refers to ideas and behaviors built from the influences we take in from our environment. By contrast, thinking "outside the box" means stepping beyond these influences to generate new ideas. However, this is not an all-or-nothing proposition. While we might aim to think entirely outside the box, it's impossible to do so completely. Our thoughts require a foundation, built from what we've learned and experienced. This is why childhood is so crucial: it's when we develop our capacity to think. As adults, we need to accept and challenge these mental boxes to find balance and growth. The best ideas arise when we use what we've learned inside the box to create new perspectives beyond it. This is where the continuum of thinking outside the box becomes most valuable.

To think outside the box more often, we must reconfigure our current patterns of thinking. This requires stepping away from distractions. For instance, when we watch TV, listen to music, or scroll social media, we are living inside someone else's box. These creators profit from our engagement, which is not inherently bad, but it's important to ask whether we are also profiting—mentally, emotionally, or spiritually. The decision to rearrange our thinking patterns is the first step toward thinking outside the box and living more authentically.

I (Robert) often ask people, "What percentage of your day do you spend living in someone else's mind?" Initially, most people misunderstand the question. They might say, "I don't live in anyone else's mind." But when I rephrase it as, "What percentage of your day do you spend living in someone else's world?" the realization sets in. Many realize they spend more time than they thought—watching, listening to, and consuming content created by others. Living in our own world—thinking independently—is living outside the box.

It is important to strike a balance between inside– and outside–the–box thinking. Thinking inside the box allows for communication and cooperation; it makes teamwork and society possible. However, staying inside the box all the time can trap us in a worker-bee mentality, leaving us dissatisfied and stagnant. On the other hand, living entirely outside the box can isolate us, making it difficult to connect with others or function in the world. Divine innocence enables us to find harmony between these extremes.

For neurodivergent individuals, living outside the box often comes naturally. Their unique perspectives are a facet of their divine innocence. For others, thinking outside the box requires deliberate effort. For instance, if we work a traditional job, we are living in our boss's box during work hours. That's part of the agreement. However, if we feel trapped, it is crucial to recognize this dynamic and decide whether it serves us. The key is understanding the boxes we live in and how they align with our goals and values.

Builders, Boxes, and the Wolf

Builders living in divine innocence expand their mental boxes when they feel confined, but they never abandon their foundation. They adapt, learning new skills or starting new ventures to meet their needs without betraying their core identity. By contrast, the ignorant builder either clings to the same box, refusing all change, or abandons their box entirely, searching for something better. Both responses invite the wolf—ignorance—into their lives.

The ignorant builder who resists change may avoid disaster for a time but lives a stagnant, lonely existence. When the wolf inevitably arrives—through illness, hardship, or other challenges—their rigidity leads to regret. Conversely, the ignorant builder who abandons their box is always searching for greener pastures but never finds peace. They are trapped in a cycle of dissatisfaction and disconnection.

The divinely innocent builder understands that their box protects and empowers them. When they feel the need for change, they expand their box rather than rejecting it. This might mean starting a new hobby, learning a new skill, or exploring a new perspective. They remain grounded in their divine innocence, seeking peace and growth without losing their foundation.

As you journey through this book, you will learn how to embrace your divine innocence and apply it to your builder type. Whether you are a stick, straw, or brick builder, your divine innocence equips you to navigate the challenges of life with clarity, strength, and integrity. By understanding your mental boxes and choosing when to think inside or outside of them, you can live a balanced, fulfilling life that is true to your divine purpose.

Freedom is to Make Decisions Based in Innocence

This understanding of your builder type and divine innocence sets the foundation for exploring how these principles interact with the wolves we encounter in life. To illustrate this interaction, let me share a deeply personal story that reveals how embracing divine innocence can transform even the most painful experiences into a source of strength and purpose.

Unable to speak until I (Robert) was nearly five years old, I immersed myself in constructing an inner world, a sanctuary within my mind. Looking back, I see how that world was not just a refuge but a blueprint for the life I would build. It was a fortress, shielding me from the harshness of the outside world. My brothers, along with others around me, mocked and belittled me, fueled by the narrative my mother created. They justified their cruelty because they had surrendered their own innocence to her influence. My mother was the wolf behind closed doors, orchestrating the atmosphere of our home.

Even my father, though he did not actively join her rejections, sacrificed his innocence in a bid to maintain peace.

The fort I built in my mind, though invisible to others, insulated me from these external forces. However, as I grew, I came to understand that while insulation could protect me, isolation would ultimately defeat me. I realized at ten years old that to flourish, I had to engage with the world. My inner sanctuary could provide strength, but I needed to extend my life outward, to build something real in the physical world.

Although I did not fully understand the definition of success at that young age, I had an intuitive sense of its formula. Through the lens of autism, I chose to embrace my innocence as the foundation for success, trusting that the details would reveal themselves over time. My perspective was vastly different from my mother's and brothers'. Their cruelty—the wolf's expression in children—manifested in name-calling and other forms of ignorance. Because I did not speak until I was five, my siblings called me a "retard." My mother dismissed their behavior by telling others I was simply lazy and would talk when I was ready.

But I did not start talking because I was ready. I spoke to survive. I needed a voice to protect myself from those around me, including my mother. Yet my speaking did not bring her joy. Instead, she used it as another tool for cruelty. "Can't you talk intelligently?" she would snap. "Can't you say anything that makes sense? You talk in riddles. I can't understand you." These words left me bewildered. I could not comprehend what she found so confusing—or why she did.

Her insults escalated. She would say in front of others, "I wish I never had him. I should have left him in the cart at the department store." Or worse: "I should have drowned him in the tub when I had the chance. He always gets mad at that one." When I realized she relished provoking my anger, I decided not to give her that power anymore. Her tactics were designed to assert dominance, a hallmark of the wolf within her.

I knew I was not the "retard" my brothers labeled me, and I chose to ignore their taunts. My mother, the proverbial wolf in sheep's clothing, had transformed my brothers into her minions. Yet even as I endured her attacks, I learned from them. If you survive the wolf's blows, it becomes a harsh teacher, imparting lessons you cannot learn otherwise. My mother's treatment of me pushed me to become someone of significance. Her wolfishness became the fuel for my determination.

This dynamic is a stark reminder of how the actions of those close to us can steer us away from innocence. In my case, autism acted as a filter, preserving my innocence in the face of relentless negativity. Where others might require years of therapy to rediscover their innocence, my autistic lens gave me the emotional distance to retain it. Autism protected me from the social pressures that so often strip people of their authenticity.

Rather than conforming to those pressures, I used them as tools for learning and growth. One of the unintended lessons my mother taught me was the importance of speaking intelligently. Over time, I realized that speaking intelligently was only half the equation. Listening intelligently was just as crucial. I had to hone this skill to survive in her presence.

Learning to "speak intelligently" in a way others could understand was no small feat. My thoughts, processed through the unique lens of autism, often emerged as what my mother derisively called "riddles." In my view, they were expressions of verbal eloquence—my own language. These so-called riddles were part of the fort I had built to protect myself. Yet I recognized the need to step outside that fort and communicate in a world that required clarity without sacrificing my divine innocence.

Through this journey, I learned that maintaining divine innocence does not mean retreating into isolation. It means engaging with the world authentically, holding onto the truth of who we are while navigating the complexities of life with strength and grace.

The Mantle of Innocence: A Shield and a Guide

My innocence saved me. It became my guide, teaching me how to navigate an unfriendly world. I chose to find value within myself and to create a meaningful life despite my mother's intentional or unintentional desire to discard me. Some might look at my life and call it a success. For me, success feels elusive. The fact that I am still here feels more like a miracle than an achievement. If innocence has its own soul—and I believe it does—it wrapped me in its protective mantle. That protection is why I could not let failure win. I had to learn what success truly meant and how to achieve it.

My innocence taught me to see two things about my mother for which I am grateful: she gave me life, and she did not take it away.

In my earliest days, I learned to observe the world without the added pressure of speaking intelligently. As an adult, I now strive to express myself clearly, though I still worry about having to explain myself without my riddles. As a child, feeling devalued became a driving force. I used those negative experiences to shape a positive outlook as an adult. I learned to value others deeply. I studied people, observing their worth from my state of innocence. Through this process, I not only recognized my own value but also became adept at helping others see theirs.

This has had an interesting side effect: I became addicted to feeling valued by others. Today, people might call me a people pleaser, but that label misses the mark. I am not driven by the need to please; I am a value seeker. I find worth in others and help them express it through their innocence.

It is a delicate balance between my innocence and my interactions with others, including you, dear reader. Part of me feels the need to explain myself in greater detail, to strip away the riddles so you do not have to decipher them. This creates a tension within me, but it is the nature of my autistic mind. I write from a place of innocence, accessing the purest parts of my thoughts. Unlike many, I do not judge myself harshly for this. Autism is not a handicap or a mental illness in my eyes; it is simply my truth. For me, thinking in innocence is my normal.

That said, any gift—be it intelligence, beauty, talent, fame, wealth, charisma, or spirituality—becomes a curse if we view it outside the lens of innocence. Even personality itself, without innocence, can be a burden. Any such curse is an open door for the wolf to blow down our house. While some see autism as a curse, I see it as an immeasurable blessing. Autism, to me, embodies humility, which is the conscious expression of divine innocence. I am fortunate to have a patient editor who sifts through my riddles to ensure that what I write connects with you.

If I had not made decisions rooted in divine innocence, anger, hatred, or bitterness might have consumed me. Carrying those negative emotions would have drained my energy and trapped me in a cycle of hopelessness. Negative feelings belong to the wolf; they exhaust us and squander the precious opportunities of each day. Divine innocence, however, reframes each day as a unique gift—a present to be treasured. While feelings like anger and sadness are natural reactions to pain, we must transform those negatives into positives as soon as we can.

Divine innocence liberated me from my mother's manipulation and helped me see her beauty despite the abuse. In hindsight, I see how autism was a blessing. It allowed me to maintain clarity and preserve my sense of self amidst an abusive upbringing. This same innocence can free all of us from manipulation, whether it comes from parents, institutions, workplaces, or others. When we deny our divine innocence, we compromise our truth and integrity. The world's relentless barrage of ideas about who we are can make us question our value. Yet, we always have a choice: we can return to innocence, staying true to ourselves and finding peace. In doing so, we become beacons of light for others. If we do not, we risk being consumed by depression, anxiety, or harmful coping mechanisms like addiction. Worse still, we become vulnerable to the wolves around us—be they individuals, corporations, governments, or the media.

At ten years old, my brother's innocence saved my life. Following an emotional breakdown triggered by my mother's abuse, I was overcome by despair. She had punched me in the face for something I did not do, and the weight of her rejection crushed me. Feeling unloved and betrayed, I wanted to die. The wolf within me turned its destructive nature inward. I grabbed a knife from the kitchen and stormed into my brother Billy's room—the brother who hated me most —demanding he kill me. To my surprise, Billy laughed and refused. In that moment, despite his usual wolfish tendencies, he chose innocence.

Billy's refusal left me at a crossroads. Lacking the resolve to harm myself, I had to decide whether to continue living in despair or to search for a way to transform the negativity around me. That decision marked a turning point. My mother's hatred and my brother's unexpected choice not to engage with my wolfish plea set the stage for my transformation.

This moment became foundational. The despair born of my mother's hatred brought me to the brink of death, but Billy's innocent response forced me to make a new choice. I began to embrace my divine innocence, drawing strength from it. This meant cherishing the unique perspective through which I viewed the world. Many years later, I would learn that this perspective was labeled "autistic" by society. Autism, far from being a limitation, served as my shield, preserving my divine innocence and protecting the essence of who I was created to be.

Most people who hear my story ask how I avoided ending up dead, imprisoned, or addicted to drugs. The answer is straightforward: my divine innocence sustained me. It kept me alive and gave me the strength to persevere, even when life felt unbearable. It has never been easy, but life does not promise ease. What I know with certainty is that without my divine innocence, my life would have been infinitely harder. Through it, I discovered freedom, resilience, and the ability to transform even the darkest moments into opportunities for growth.

For each of us, the key to transforming negatives into positives and remaining in our divine innocence lies in staying true to the essence of who God created us to be. If we are born autistic, that part of us deserves honor and love. If we are naturally extroverted and thrive in the company of others, we must embrace that energy. If we are reserved and yearn for the serenity of the woods over the buzz of the big city, we should cherish that about ourselves. Being true to our unique design is the foundation of divine innocence because that truth is our home—our soul's essence.

I hold a theory that long before we take our first breath—before we are even a glimmer in our father's eye—we existed as unspent energy in a realm untouched by earthly influences. In this space of consciousness, our spirits prepare with a pure heart to embody a divinely innocent and beautiful form. When we arrive in this life, naked and vulnerable, someone inevitably counts our fingers and toes and exclaims that we are "perfect." For that moment, at least, we are seen in the light of our divine innocence, unable to be anything but purely ourselves—free of guile, malice, or pretense.

This divine essence is immediately recognizable. When children enter our lives, their unique personalities shine through from the start. These personalities are not malleable; they are stable and enduring traits that remain with us throughout life, and perhaps beyond. While these personalities can be polluted by external influences, their core remains untouched, waiting for us to return to it whenever we stray.

As children grow and develop the ability to make choices, they face the most profound decision of all: will they build a life centered on harmony, rooted in divine innocence, or will they surrender to ignorance, becoming a wolf who tears down instead of builds? This choice—between creating a home in divine innocence or roaming as a destructive wolf—shapes not only their lives but the world around them.

Divine innocence is a powerful, stable state that we can always return to, even if we have wandered far from it. However, this return is not automatic or permanent. It requires deliberate reflection and intentional healing. The journey back to innocence is ongoing because the wolf—both within and without—constantly seeks to knock down the doors of our souls.

The wolf is not always easy to recognize. Sometimes, it masquerades as something familiar and trusted, as in the story of *Little Red Riding Hood*. Red's innocence, expressed through curiosity and questioning, enabled her to discern that the figure before her was not her beloved grandmother but the wolf in disguise. Her questions saved her life. Similarly, in our own lives, we may confront loved ones who have temporarily lost touch with their divine innocence and succumbed to ignorance. In such moments, we must remain steadfast in our own divine innocence, refusing to open the door to the wolf— no matter how familiar its guise.

At other times, the wolf manifests within us, and recognizing it is even more challenging. Personality is pervasive and often invisible to ourselves. It colors our perceptions and interactions, making it difficult to see when we have drifted from our true nature. We may unknowingly adopt wolfish traits by conforming to the expectations or influences of others—whether parents, teachers, or peers. Over time, these external influences can obscure our access to the truth of who we are.

Parents and caregivers, for instance, can unintentionally or deliberately erode a child's innocence. Some parents impose their unfulfilled dreams onto their children, seeking to remake them in their own image or using them to vicariously experience what they feel they missed. While guiding children is a natural part of parenting, imposing rigid expectations can lead them away from their divine innocence, leaving them burdened with unmet expectations and confusion about their true selves. Parenting in divine innocence, on the other hand, involves celebrating the unique brilliance of each child. From the moment of their birth, we can see their intelligence, vitality, and individuality. Babies arrive with a soul-deep wisdom that is often more profound than we, as parents, can immediately comprehend. The challenge and privilege of parenting lie in discovering and honoring their distinct wiring—their personality and purpose—and helping them feel valued for exactly who they are.

As children, we naturally navigate a process of losing our divine innocence as the earthly journey overtakes the purity of the consciousness we once had. This transformation continues when we transition to the role of parents, shaping the next generation. For some, however, there is a protective layer that slows or even halts this process, particularly in children with what society labels as "special needs" or "mental disorders." If you have an autistic-minded child or one with other unique cognitive traits like Down's Syndrome, consider yourself fortunate. These so-called disorders act as guardians of divine innocence, shielding the child's mind from the outer world's expectations as they grow into adulthood. For example, individuals with conditions like Down's Syndrome often exhibit an enduring innocence, untainted by societal pressures. This is similar to the protective mechanism seen in autism, where the mind retains its connection to divine innocence. When these abilities and perspectives are recognized and understood by those without such traits, the vast potential of the human mind becomes clearer.

Autism, while presenting challenges in communication and relationships, serves a remarkable protective role. Its distinct way of processing the world shields divine innocence from the relentless attacks of the wolf. This protective function is something everyone needs, regardless of whether they have autism or not. Those without this natural mantle of protection are more vulnerable to external influences that can distort their sense of self, pulling them away from who God created them to be. Unfortunately, it took nearly half a century and much introspection for me to fully appreciate my own diagnosis of autism. For a long time, I resisted it, viewing the label as a judgment that implied I was somehow "broken." I could not see how such a diagnosis could benefit me or those I loved. Now, I understand that this diagnosis was not for my benefit alone; it was for those around me—and for you, the reader. Through this realization, I have come to see autism as a unique gift, one that offers a pathway to stand firmly in divine innocence.

My goal is to help you reclaim your divine innocence, whether it was taken from you in childhood through circumstances beyond your control or whether it became misplaced due to trauma or societal conditioning. Through understanding and embracing this journey, we can find a way back to the truth of who we are and live in alignment with our divine purpose. By recognizing the divine innocence in ourselves and others, we can navigate these challenges with clarity and grace, always returning to the home of our soul's truth. This is how we build lives that are resilient, fulfilling, and deeply connected to the divine.

Violence is the Wolf of the Soul

In light of what we now know about the wolf and the three little pigs, let us consider why the adage "never talk about religion, politics, or money" is problematic. Yes, these topics can be contentious, but they profoundly shape and change our lives, whether we like it or not. To avoid them entirely is like sticking our fingers in our ears and chanting, "La, la, la, la, la." This is not a time in history to be uninformed or apathetic—if such a time has ever existed. Those who choose ignorance or apathy allow the wolf to creep into their souls through neglect, whether they realize it or not. To deny the wolf's presence is to invite it to take over, subtly undermining our innocence until it drives us to actions that betray who we truly are.

By contrast, staying informed about the world—despite its violence—can strengthen and protect our divine innocence. By engaging with the world in a state of innocence, we can discern truth from falsehood and reject manipulation by the media or the powers that be. If we find that we have succumbed to the wolf, either through aggression or neglect, we must invite innocence back into our souls. Innocence restores our power and influence, even during violent times. Though it may seem counterintuitive, our true strength lies in our innocence. As we delve deeper into this idea, you will see this truth unfold.

We must remain vigilant against the wolf without becoming it. Like the wolf in *The Three Little Pigs*, it waits for any opportunity to blow down our house and devour us. The wolf is especially active in the realms of religion, politics, and money. If we do not stay rooted in innocence, we risk becoming refugees in our own souls, wandering lost and disconnected.

Because the world operates outside the bounds of innocence, it is crucial that we remain steadfast in our own. We achieve this by relying on intuition and focusing on our innocence in every situation. Disagreements about religion, politics, or money—or any topic, really—are not the true problem. The real problem lies in how we handle those disagreements. When we act outside of innocence, we unleash the wolf within us or provoke it in others.

When someone's wolf comes howling at our door, we face a choice. We can release our own wolf and escalate the battle, or we can remain in innocence and invite a miracle to unfold. Most of us instinctively respond to another's wolf with our own, mistakenly believing it will protect us. In truth, releasing our wolf denies our divine nature, distances us from God, and abandons the home of our soul. This leaves us lost, purposeless, and destructive, attacking anything or anyone in our path.

By contrast, when we remain within the bounds of innocence, we stay connected to our power and influence. While we may need to develop the skills to respond more effectively to the wolves we encounter, we must never abandon our innocence. It is our greatest strength and our truest home.

Innocence Nourishes the Universe

When we step outside of our core personality, we step away from our divine innocence. At the heart of our innocence lies the inner self—our true essence, the unique being God created us to be. This inner self is invaluable, beyond measure, and infinitely precious. To live in integrity with our innocence is to remain true to this inner self, which is the wellspring of both our personality and character.

Personality and character, though often confused, are distinct aspects of who we are. Personality is the stable, unchanging blueprint of how we are wired. It is the purest expression of our innocence and inner self. While personality itself does not change throughout our lifetime, its expression can adapt based on the people in our lives and the circumstances we face. Our perceptions of our own personality are often influenced by how others react to us and by the environment we navigate.

Character, by contrast, is the bridge between our personality and the world around us. It is the medium through which we relate to others. Rooted in the innocence of our inner self, character develops over time in response to external influences like caregivers, siblings, friends, media, and the broader environment. When character is true to its divine anchor in innocence, it fosters genuine connections, linking the purity of one person's soul with another's.

While personality remains constant, the way we express it grows and evolves. Similarly, our understanding of character matures as we encounter life's challenges and influences. These experiences shape the choices we make, often distorting or even damaging the core values inherent in our inner self. Many of us struggle to express ourselves purely because we feel judged, misunderstood, or rejected by others' flawed expressions of their own personalities and characters. This is the essence of what we call *the wolf cycle*—a concept we will explore further later.

Divine innocence serves as a shield for the mind, radiating a godly aura. To live in innocence is to fully inhabit the present moment, unburdened by worldly limitations, and driven by the belief that anything is possible. Innocence allows us to participate in life authentically, without comparison or fear. It is not a future destination; it is an active state of being. Through innocence, we embrace our relevance and let our character manifest freely and completely.

In life's relationships—whether with children, spouses, or close friends—we often create an "assumptive environment." In these environments, we unconsciously project our personalities, builder traits, and values onto others, treating our perspectives as absolute truths rather than subjective perceptions. While usually unintentional, this projection can steer others' destinies away from their divine innocence, replacing their true path with our own misguided dreams. Such actions not only harm their innocence but also erode our own.

The purpose of this book is to help you identify and respect the core values, behaviors, and thought processes of yourself and others. By understanding these distinctions, you can learn how to collaborate with others instead of dominating or manipulating them. You will also discover how to establish divinely innocent boundaries, ensuring that your own needs and values are honored. These insights can be applied to every relationship in your life—whether with children, spouses, business partners, friends, or family members. Furthermore, they can guide you in healing old wounds, even those tied to individuals who are no longer present in your life.

The concept of *the wolf cycle* is designed to help you navigate and understand why people behave the way they do. This book, as a result of that work, is intended to help you discern your own character without imposing it onto others. At the same time, it equips you to separate others' imposed characters from your own, freeing you to live fully in alignment with your divine innocence.

Enter the Three Little Pigs. Stage Right.

To embrace the theory in this book, the first step is to reject the idea that the brick-building pig is inherently superior, as the original story suggests. Instead, we must understand that each of the three pigs built their house according to their personality traits. These traits, shaped by their unique brain wiring, influenced their values and ways of being in the world. Their choices were expressions of their divine innocence.

Each pig had specific reasons for building the type of house they did, and these reasons were unrelated to whether a wolf might destroy their homes. If they had known about the wolf ahead of time, building as they did would have been an act of self-sabotage. But no one had taught them about the wolf, and even if they had been warned, their choices likely would not have changed. Their building materials reflected their innate personalities—their divine innocence. As we will explore, the problem was never the materials themselves but how they were used to construct the houses. Furthermore, the world needs all three builder types—straw, stick, and brick—because each contributes unique gifts, abilities, and perspectives to society. Even the wolf plays a crucial role in helping the pigs' community build stronger, more resilient structures after the initial disasters.

A central truth about the wolf must also be understood: the wolf exists within all of us, and it is one of our most valuable teachers. In the story of the three little pigs, the wolf taught important lessons to the villagers, but they failed to recognize its value. They feared the wolf, viewing it only as a threat to be avoided, rather than as a critical teacher. To remain in our divine innocence, we must not follow the villagers' example.

Hindsight often compels foresight, but only when self-indulgent regret transforms into understanding. Consider the original story of the three pigs. The first pig, whose house of straw was blown down, left descendants who said, "We must never build with straw again, or we will die." Similarly, the second pig's descendants rejected sticks, and the brick pig's descendants clung to the safety of their bricks, fearing to venture outside. These conclusions were misguided. The issue was never the materials but how they were chosen and used. The straw pig's descendants needed to realize that straw wasn't the problem—it was the type of straw and the method of construction. The same was true for the stick pig's descendants. Even the brick pig's descendants, while safe, had to overcome their fear-induced isolation, as their house became a self-imposed prison.

When asked which house they would choose to build, most people pick the brick house because the fairytale positions it as the only safe option. This communal hindsight reflects a reaction rooted in fear rather than thoughtful understanding. Safety, while important, is not a core value; it is a reactionary concept often driven by fear. And fear— whether valid or imagined—can become the antidote to freedom, as demonstrated by the brick-building pig.

The building materials of the pigs are not interchangeable because they represent each pig's core personality—their unique wiring. The straw pig (Rob) needed to use straw, the stick pig (Bob) needed to use sticks, and the brick pig (Bobbie) needed to use bricks. If any of the pigs had chosen a different material, they would have betrayed their true selves, violating their innocence and committing acts of self-betrayal. The same holds true for us. Choosing the wrong building material leads to creating a home for our souls that is misaligned with our core personalities. This conflict results in misunderstandings, tension, and traumatic experiences for ourselves and those around us.

The process of sifting through life's traumas enables us to discover our true selves. When we transform past regrets into understanding, we gain the clarity needed to heal wounded hearts and foster mutual insight. This healing empowers us to prevent future trauma in our relationships with our children, our communities, and ourselves.

The Wolf Was Not Toxic...and Neither Are Our Least Favorite People

It is not easy to work with or live alongside someone from a different builder group. Rob, the straw pig, struggles to live with his brother Bob, the stick pig, and vice versa. Never mind Bobbie, the brick pig, who happens to think her house is the best of all.

Too often, we label people who are different from us as toxic...or they label us that way. However, 'toxic' is not a valid concept of divine innocence. The term toxicity exists only in the wolf's vernacular. Anyone who stands in the wolf's way is 'toxic,' and that becomes his excuse to attack.

We will say it again: 'toxic' is a wolfish term. The reality is that people (or we) are not toxic. Instead, we are misunderstood—either by others or by ourselves–or simply different. To call someone 'toxic' is to declare them poisonous or harmful, even to the point of feeling that they are a threat to our survival. When we apply this term to people, we impose self-righteous, self-centered judgments about what is 'good' or 'bad,' judgments that are not grounded in truth. They are not founded in divine innocence. These judgments are rooted in the wolf's predatory instinct to dominate and control.

In truth, what we often call 'toxic' is often a misunderstanding of someone's divine innocence, their true personality. Even if that person is a wolf, the divinely innocent mind will not label them as 'toxic.' By using this label, we become the wolf ourselves.

This is a critical point to understand. As we move through life, we must take the time to reflect and ask ourselves, 'When am I the wolf? When am I seeking to control or dominate someone rather than trying to understand them?'

The drive to control or dominate another person is wolfish, yet this is the only purpose of a label like 'toxic.' Even the wolf is not toxic. He is dangerous, perhaps, and requires our thoughtful and measured response, but we must remember that we are always safe from his attacks. When we remain in divine innocence, in the home of our soul, the wolf cannot harm us. He becomes a passing experience rather than a toxic one, leaving our soul and core identity intact.

The straw, the stick, and the brick represent three fundamental sets of core values and personality traits. This is why there is no single "correct" answer to the question of which house the three little pigs should have built. All three houses—and the personalities they represent—are equally valid and true.

The way we answer the question, 'Which house would you build?' reveals much about how we internally process and respond to life's challenges, including behaviors, religion, traumatic experiences, autism, personal beliefs, identity decisions, bullying, environment, and even parenting. It also offers insight into how we react to encountering the wolf and how we attempt to protect ourselves from him.

CHAPTER 2

THE WOLF HAS NO HOME

The wolf is not always a four-legged creature. It manifests in the wind and weather, in the actions of those around us, in the limitations of our bodies, or even in the thoughts that occupy our minds. In moments of despair, overwhelming heartache, undiagnosed mental illness, or broken-spiritedness, we often make irrational decisions. Feeling attacked by external forces, we respond by attacking—either others or ourselves. In these moments, we become the wolf. We lose sight of our true nature, our divine innocence, and in an effort to escape our pain, we mentally and emotionally abandon our own souls. We no longer want to be ourselves, as being ourselves feels synonymous with suffering.

This cycle of pain leads to aggression—toward others or inwardly toward ourselves. In these moments, we adopt the wolf's nature. We abandon the sanctuary of our souls, accepting the wolf into our hearts. With this decision, formed in response to fear and pain, the wolf emerges within us. Yet the wolf discovers a painful truth: homelessness is far more agonizing than living in a besieged home. The homeless wolf is desperate and sets out to claim a home. Spotting a pig nearby, the wolf attacks, hoping to drive the pig out and claim the house for himself. To succeed, the wolf must convince the pig to leave willingly, manipulating him with the appearance of strength and inevitability. With his huffing and puffing, the wolf's goal is to sow doubt and fear in the pig, forcing him to abandon his home.

But the pig, standing firm in his divine innocence, refuses. With a resolute, "Not by the hair of my chinny-chin-chin," the pig protects his home. The wolf's intent, his motives, and his seemingly unrelenting confidence must always be questioned.

If the wolf succeeds in driving the pig out, he occupies the home but is never at peace. The wolf becomes a squatter, forever uncomfortable and aware that this house does not belong to him. He knows he does not truly belong, even if others forget this fact. Meanwhile, the displaced pig becomes a wandering wolf in search of a new home, perpetuating the cycle.

What does this look like in our daily lives? Reflect on an innocent conversation or a budding relationship that began with sincerity. Then recall how anger, fear, or hurt feelings crept in, derailing that connection. The wolf was at the door. The question is: in that moment, did you stand firm in your divine innocence and keep the wolf at bay? Or did you succumb to the wolf's influence, attacking or lashing out? Perhaps you initiated the conflict, donning the mantle of the wolf from the start. Whatever the case, these moments are opportunities for reflection.

The wolf blindsides us, turning calm into chaos, leaving us wondering, "What went wrong? It wasn't supposed to be this way." Yet the wolf always gives warning—through a howl, a growl, or the huffing and puffing that herald his intent. His goal is to invade, redirecting what should have been a peaceful moment into one of hostility, anger, or despair.

Once his fangs are bared and claws unsheathed, the wolf's intent becomes unmistakable. He whispers into our minds, "Let me in, or I'll destroy everything you've built. I'll take over your house, your peace, your life." Despair, hurtful words, destructive behavior, suicidal thoughts, or reckless deeds often follow, bringing his whispers to life. If you open the door, flee out the back, or allow the wolf to overpower a poorly built home, he moves in. The house, once a sanctuary, now becomes his lair.

When friendships sour, communities fall apart, or harmony turns to discord, it is often due to anger rooted in pain and fear—manifestations of the wolf's huffing and puffing.

The wolf's howl grows louder as he seeks to dominate the hearts of men. His intent is clear: to make himself comfortable in a home that is not his own. Unless the pig clings to the protective mantle of divine innocence, the wolf will persist. Even after succeeding in displacing the pig, the wolf remains restless. He knows he is a trespasser, forever insecure in his stolen home. To maintain his position, he relies on manipulation, domination, and aggression, perpetuating his destruction.

The wolf does not care if his harm becomes permanent. His goal is prominence, no matter the cost. Beware of his tactics and stand firm in your divine innocence.

When we let the wolf in and allow ourselves to be displaced, we are acting in ignorance of a profound truth: our home is our soul. Our soul is divine innocence, comprised of pure love, and within it lies the strength and capacity to refocus our minds on what is true and what is love. At any moment, we can choose to kick the wolf out. Yet, we often fail to realize this. When we falter, we forget this truth, act out of ignorance, and lose sight of our true nature. In doing so, we abandon our home and go searching for one outside of ourselves.

As wolves, we project our pain of homelessness onto others, often by demonizing them. This projection stems from our internal anguish, temporarily easing the pain within our souls. It may take many forms—focusing on the flaws of others, manipulating, deceiving, expressing anger, passing judgment, or acting self-righteously. These attacks, whether in word or deed, serve as a desperate attempt to drive away the despair we feel. In essence, when we lash out, we are huffing and puffing at someone else's door, hungry for a sense of belonging and desperate to feel at home in the world.

"Our home is our soul. Our soul is divine innocence."

But why do we feel this despair in the first place? It is because we have abandoned our souls to an experience, a feeling, or a belief. In doing so, we abandon the only true home we have on this earth. At its core, this projected despair is the soul's belief that it is homeless. The homeless soul wanders aimlessly, searching for a place to call its own. And in this wandering, it sees others at home in their souls. Fueled by jealousy and rage, the homeless soul attempts to steal or destroy the homes of others. Just as the wolf in the story roams from house to house, trying to blow down the pigs' homes, the homeless soul seeks to penetrate and overtake the homes of others, leaving devastation in its wake.

The wolf's attacks have significant impacts on the pigs. When the wolf targets a pig's house, it brings the home under siege. In these moments, the pig—a person living in divine innocence—has the power to choose how they will respond. There are three possible responses to the wolf's attack:

1. The pig abandons their home: The wolf is allowed in, and the pig, believing their home is lost, leaves in search of a new one. In this moment, the pig becomes the wolf, continuing the cycle of destruction.

2. The pig rebuilds their home: The wolf is allowed in, and although destruction occurs, the pig remains in divine innocence. They choose to learn from the experience, rebuild

their home stronger than before, and grow through the process of healing and overcoming.

3. The pig stands strong: The pig refuses to let the wolf in, standing firm at the door despite the wolf's huffing and puffing. By remaining rooted in their divine innocence, they prevent any damage to their home.

In the first two scenarios, the wolf gains entry either by the pig opening the door or by the wolf's forceful efforts. In everyday life, this plays out in various ways. We may feel victimized by the wolf's attack, take it personally, or ruminate over their actions or words. We might even believe the harmful things the wolf says about us. In doing so, we effectively allow the wolf to blow down our house. Worse, we open the door, letting the wolf in to take up residence and wreak havoc within. This creates the belief that we no longer have a home of our own, that our soul has been penetrated and destroyed by the wolf.

These feelings leave us in despair, consumed by pain and a sense of vulnerability and loneliness. But the critical question remains: What is our response to these feelings?

The Pig Who Leaves Home and Becomes the Wolf

In the first scenario, we abandon our home to the wolf and set out in search of a new one. When we come across another pig's home, we find ourselves at their door, projecting our despair and rage over our homelessness. We huff and puff, attempting to blow their house down.

This pig, now under siege, faces the same choice we did when the wolf came to our door. If this pig chooses to leave their home and search for another, they too become the wolf, and the cycle continues.

At some point, however, the pig-turned-wolf can pause and recognize what they have become. They can realize that they have taken on the wolf's nature and choose to make a different decision. They can wake up to the truth: they already have a home and have had it all along. Like Dorothy in *The Wizard of Oz*, when Glinda the Good Witch reveals that she had the power to return home all along, the wolf can awaken from their ignorance. In that moment, the wolf returns to their divine innocence—their true pig nature. They choose to go back to their home, even though it may be damaged and in need of repair, and begin the process of rebuilding. By doing so, they end the wolf cycle and reclaim their divine innocence.

This is precisely what happened to Dorothy. In Kansas, her conflict with Mrs. Gulch over Toto leads her to leave the home of her soul and become the wolf. She lashes out, runs away, and begins searching for something she believes is missing. Through her dream in the Land of Oz, Dorothy learns a profound truth: she has only one true home, and it has always been there waiting for her. Notably, Dorothy's outward appearance does not change; she still looks like the sweet teenage girl we first meet. But during her time in Oz, she embodies the wolf, living in ignorance of her soul and her home. When she breaks the wolf cycle of destruction that Mrs. Gulch's ignorance initiated, she returns to her divine innocence. She goes back to Kansas, embraces her family with apologies, love, and joy, and brings newfound peace and harmony to those around her.

In real life, breaking the wolf cycle can take many forms. It may look like an addict whose parents were addicts but who decides to end the cycle and seek help. It could be a boss who recognizes how belittling their employees is damaging both morale and productivity, and who commits to learning a new communication style. It might be a spouse who realizes they have been dismissing their partner's needs while manipulating their partner to meet their own, and who makes a conscious effort to change their behavior.

In each of these examples, the wolf cycle ends the moment the individual wakes up to their ignorance, returns to their divine innocence, and makes the choice to rebuild their home rather than destroy another's. It is a courageous and transformative act that restores harmony and rekindles the joy and love inherent in divine innocence.

The Pig Whose Home is Destroyed But Chooses to Rebuild

In the second scenario, we respond to the wolf's attack by assessing the damage to our homes—our souls—and choosing to rebuild and strengthen the structure. In this process, we may need to expel the wolf if we had opened the door to him, or we may simply need to rebuild after he has blown our house down. Either way, we initially feel despair, but we make the conscious choice to process that despair within the broken walls of our souls, refusing to become the wolf ourselves.

In everyday life, the first step is to acknowledge what has happened. This does not mean dwelling on the pain indefinitely, but rather recognizing the damage done to our souls. We must grieve. We must process our pain and trauma to set ourselves on the path to healing. In my life, this required revisiting my past and the traumatic experiences of my upbringing, which ultimately led to the creation of my first book, *Stop Your Crying.* By writing about these experiences and my healing journey, I (Robert) hoped to encourage others to face and overcome their pain, thereby rebuilding their souls.

Once we have acknowledged the damage, we have the opportunity to rebuild through our own divine innocence. This means allowing our experiences to shape us into stronger, wiser, and more compassionate individuals. We must resist the tendency to remain victims or to dwell on the belief that "I have been through too much, and I cannot move past this." Instead, we must embrace what has happened, find its value, and allow it to make us better rather than bitter. The truth is that the pain will not go away until we face it.

The other truth about pain is that the more we resist it, the more it intensifies and the greater the damage it causes. The only real way to rid ourselves of pain is to relax into it. When we allow pain to flow through us, it dissipates. If we clench up and resist, it remains trapped in our system. This is why a bird can sit on an active electrical wire without harm, while a grounded human would be electrocuted. Ungrounded electricity causes no damage. Similarly, this is why a drunk driver in a head-on collision is more likely to survive without injury than their victim. The drunk driver, lacking tension in their muscles, is less impacted by the collision. The same principle applies to the palm tree, which bends in a hurricane and withstands the storm better than the brittle oak.

The next time you feel emotional pain, try this: close your eyes, feel the pain, and relax into it. As you allow yourself to fully experience the pain, you will likely find that it flows through you and dissipates.

Furthermore, there is immense value in pain. When we allow ourselves to see the value in our pain, we turn the negatives in our lives into positives. This is not always a quick process, and it is natural to have questions about why we suffered as we did. Why did the wolf choose our house? Why were we born into a den full of wolves? These are hard questions, especially when we reflect on the sweetness and innocence of our childhood selves and wonder how such terrible things could have happened to us.

For me, the answer lay in finding the art within my pain. Even as a ten-year-old boy, I found a way to dream and build in response to my suffering. If we can step through our pain and turn it into art, we create something truly beautiful. This process goes far beyond pretending the pain does not exist or denying the past. My books are a representation of my pain as works of art. Without those painful experiences, I would have nothing meaningful to say. We all have the power to create, to overcome, and to transform. Every one of us possesses this ability. When we turn the pain of our past into art, we transform devastation into a unique superpower.

This transformation is part of the natural law of the universe. Every gardener knows that fertile soil is necessary for growth, and what fertilizes soil? Excrement. To rebuild a better house—a stronger, wiser soul that is impervious to the wolf's attacks—we must take the pain we have experienced and transform it into something beautiful.

If we fail to face and transform our pain, we spiral downward and become the martyred wolf, turning on ourselves. To avoid this outcome, we must eventually come to pity the wolf. The wolf is nothing more than a beautiful, divinely innocent pig who has abandoned their home. They cannot see their own divine innocence. They do not harness their incredible power to create beauty from their pain. Instead, they believe they are homeless. They believe their soul provides no solace, no peace, and no joy. In their ignorance, they approach another's door and demand: *"Little pig, little pig, let me in, or I will huff, and I will puff, and I will blow your house down."* It is all very sad, really.

The Pig Who Stands Strong and Says 'No Thank You'

The third choice the pig has is to stand strong in his divine innocence. Having created art from his former pain, he now has a home that is resilient enough to withstand attacks from new wolves at the door. He recognizes the strength and value of his home and knows better than to open the door to any wolf. In real life, this could be the child abuse survivor who forgives their parents and resolves to love their own children unconditionally, committing never to perpetuate the cycle of abuse.

It is crucial to acknowledge that these processes are never perfect. A parent who strives to do better after enduring a traumatic upbringing will succeed in some ways and fail in others. Their efforts, however imperfect, reflect their best attempt at breaking the cycle. Their children, in turn, face the same choice: to remain in their divine innocence and stay true to their inner pig nature or to abandon their home out of inner turmoil and become the wolf in search of another home.

Interestingly, imperfection itself is a vital aspect of divine innocence. Without imperfections, there would be no need for forgiveness, compassion, or humility—all essential elements of divine innocence. Why is imperfection a part of divine innocence? Because imperfection is an inherent truth of the human experience. Divine innocence is rooted in living authentically, and acknowledging our imperfections is an integral part of that authenticity. Only God is perfect. Our imperfections, redeemed by His love, reveal the beauty of divine grace. As long as we are alive, these imperfections will remain with us, offering us continual opportunities for growth and transformation. To believe that we can achieve perfection in this life is pure ignorance, and this misguided belief often manifests in wolfish behaviors. We have all encountered people who consider themselves perfect, and we know the havoc that attitude can cause.

The pig who remains steadfast in his divine innocence embraces both his universal human traits and his individual uniqueness. He is humbled and inspired by his imperfections, using them as opportunities for learning and self-improvement. He stands firm in his innocence even when others are rude, unkind, or hurtful. Through this process, he uncovers his gifts and talents, using them to enrich the world around him. He also begins to understand the kind of house he builds, how others build their homes, and how he can collaborate with them to create a stronger, united community, business, or family. This understanding helps him foster deeper relationships—whether in his career, family, marriage, or friendships—and provides him with the tools to remain in his divine innocence when the wolf comes knocking.

Preparing for the Chapters Ahead

In the chapters ahead, we will guide you through an exploration of the three builder types. You will undoubtedly recognize yourself and others within them. My aim is to equip you with the insights and tools needed to better understand yourself and the people you love and work with, empowering you to create a life firmly rooted in your divine innocence.

The organization of these builder chapters might seem unconventional at first, because I want to engage your imagination before delving into detailed explanations. Each chapter begins with an allegory of the builder type. My goal here is to use the power of imagination to open your mind to new possibilities—not only in your understanding of the story of the three little pigs but also in recognizing how we are divinely designed to express our personalities in innocence. These are novel concepts, and we have found that engaging the creative side of our minds can help bridge the gap between what we think we know and the realm of new ideas.

The second part of each chapter features a real-life case study from a person of that builder type. Through these stories, you will gain an inside view of the builder's mind, which is intrinsically distinct from the other types. If you share the same builder type, you may find yourself identifying with their experiences in archetypal ways. If you are a different type, their perspective may feel unfamiliar or even foreign to you. Both responses are valid and valuable as you engage with this personality theory for the first time.

Following the allegory and case study, we provide a thorough exploration of the builder's characteristics, worldview, needs, and values. To conclude each chapter, you will have the opportunity to take a self-guided quiz to determine if you align with that builder type.

As a final note, we begin with the stick builder because that is where my journey started. The stick builder is my own type, and my exploration of the types began with self-analysis. I then moved to the brick builder, which I believe reflects the personality of my former wife. For a long time, Robert struggled to see the divine innocence of the brick builder and Lara struggled to see that of the stick builder, but those are stores for another time. We end with the straw builder. This sequence also serves an additional purpose: the straw builder is the most impatient and exacting of the three, so this arrangement forces them to wait until the end to learn about themselves. If you find yourself becoming impatient as you read the following chapters, you might just be a straw builder.

We thoroughly enjoyed the process of discovering these builder types, and I hope that you do as well. May this journey deepen your understanding of yourself and others as you proceed.

CHAPTER 3
THE STICK PIG

Allegory of the Stick Pig

Mother was a saint. She was intelligent, beautiful, and all-knowing. Daddy was a good man who brought home the bacon, put food on the table, and provided a roof over our heads. I knew Daddy loved me and all of us deeply. But one day, he did not come home. Mother told us that the wolf got Daddy. His disappearance shaped my life as well as that of my two siblings.

We were triplets, born mere moments apart—Bob, Bobbie, and Rob. I was the firstborn. My name is Bob. Bobbie is my sister, and Rob is my brother.

Mother held tightly to her values, and she instilled them in us. We learned the importance of life, the necessity of hard work, and the value of resolving our differences. One constant was that we always ate together as a family. Mother often joked that we ate like pigs. I never took offense. She also taught us how to get along with others in the world.

Mother knew there might come a day when we could be taken away, just like Daddy. She made it her mission to teach us how to

85

outsmart the wolf lurking in every corner of life. As we grew older, Mother began to explain the wolf to us. She said, "The wolf is mean and nasty. He will eat you or destroy you if he can." She added, "You must outsmart the wolf all the days of your life. He will huff and puff and blow your house down if you are not careful."

I believed what Mother said about the wolf, and her warnings have stayed with me ever since. She often said, "There is a wolf looking around every corner of life. If you do not outsmart him, he will outsmart you." I understood this to mean that I could become the wolf's dinner. What I did not realize then was that the wolf could come disguised as a fellow pig, and even my own Mother carried the wolf within her.

I paid close attention to what Mother said. While I did not always agree with her views, I believed her when it came to the wolf. She taught us about the complexities of the world and the need to be intelligent and resourceful. She hoped to prepare us for long and prosperous lives. Along with kindness toward others and ourselves, she emphasized the importance of brotherly love. She taught us to stick together in times of difficulty and to value our differences. That is why I say, "Mother was a saint." God rest her chubby soul.

Mother explained how each of us was unique and how we would express ourselves in the world. She warned us that, because we built our lives with different materials, we would each face unique challenges when the wolf came knocking. And come knocking, he would. She taught us to be vigilant and prepared. If the wolf broke down our door, we needed to know how to respond. I found this idea thrilling. I felt confident I could beat the wolf and imagined myself meeting him at the door, telling him to leave. Mother cautioned me against overconfidence. Later in life, I came to understand what she meant.

Mother also told me that my ability to see value in others without pretense was a rare and precious gift. I appreciated that. I bore no malice toward others, even when they hurt me, and I was hard-pressed to keep records of wrongs. This quality bolstered my confidence and, I believe, made me likable. By refusing to harbor ill will, I found value in both positive and negative experiences. This approach gave me unique insights, strengthened my bravery, and inspired me to work hard to achieve my promises, goals, and dreams.

However, Mother warned me of the drawbacks of my open-hearted generosity. She explained that it could leave me vulnerable to the less honorable intentions of others. I might be taken advantage of by those with selfish or deceptive motives. She encouraged me to rely on my cumulative insights, which gave me the courage to survive and the ability to extract wisdom even from experiences that cost me dearly.

For instance, when someone asks for my time, money, or expertise while sharing a sob story about their struggles, they understand that my charity rarely fails. I instinctively want to help. Yet this leaves me in a heartfelt conundrum, as my willingness to assist others often comes at my own expense, which can be unhealthy. While my positive outlook and confidence enable me to help others and see value in doing so, these same traits can leave me blindsided. My tendency to fixate on solving problems sometimes leaves me vulnerable, as I feel compelled to resolve issues at any cost. This compulsion to fix can create problems of its own.

Mother's wisdom about the wolf, my nature, and the dangers of misplaced trust has been a guiding light in my life. Her teachings resonate with me even now, shaping how I navigate challenges and relationships.

Over time, I learned more about what Mother meant, and my experiences made me increasingly discerning of others' intentions. I also developed a back-up plan to mitigate the potential pitfalls of my innocent generosity. I sought out trusted advisors for second opinions, often turning to my sister Bobbie and my brother Rob for their insights. They helped me gain an objective view of situations. I valued their opinions and incorporated them alongside my own. This prudence allowed me to understand people's behavior more clearly and protect myself from being taken advantage of. Gradually, I became more refined in my judgment.

Eventually, we outgrew the tiny home Daddy had built for us. Unable to care for us any longer, Mother sent us out into the world to make our way. With tears in her eyes, she said her goodbyes, entrusting us with the values she had worked so hard to instill.

As we embarked on our individual journeys, I realized just how different my siblings and I were. My personality was governed by the value I saw in myself, others, the world, and life itself. I came to appreciate every experience, using it to organize my thoughts and better understand the strengths and gaps in my thinking. I even learned to value the wolf, as he taught me how to outwit him and navigate the systems he and his kind had created. I quickly discovered that wolves were everywhere, roaming the world to crush people's dreams.

I loved wood. I told Mother I planned to build my house out of sticks, just like my cousin had. Mother cautioned me, "Building a house out of sticks is not a good idea. It did not work out too well for your cousin." She recounted how the wolf had blown down his stick house and eaten him. Then she taught me how to build my house out of lumber, a much stronger material. I agreed with Mother. I certainly did not want to end up as the wolf's dinner.

I wanted to express my creativity and draw attention to my work. I even told Daddy before he disappeared, "I am going to build a house different from anyone else's in the world."

He replied, "There are a lot of houses out there."

I responded, "I know."

He told me, "You will have to be creative."

Daddy's words inspired me. He motivated me to think deeply and work hard. I knew that if I wanted to build a house that stood out, made a statement, and inspired others, I would need to dream big. I also realized that to achieve my vision, I had to support others in accomplishing their dreams, encouraging them to embrace their individuality and feel valued in their life choices.

As I built my home, I encountered a significant challenge: the issue of control. It was not that I wanted to control others—it was the opposite. I wanted to control myself: my environment, my actions, my thoughts, and my feelings. I wanted to ensure that I, not others, dictated the course of my life. However, I soon realized that this desire could sometimes awaken the wolf in me. In my determination to maintain control, I occasionally ended up dominating others. At other times, I grew frustrated or anxious about circumstances beyond my control, creating a destructive cycle of anxiety. Anxiety became the wolf within me, turning its feral energy inward and threatening to consume me. I knew I had to put a stop to it.

One of my workers taught me a valuable lesson about letting go of unnecessary worries. I had asked him to change something, and he said, "I will tell you what. If it keeps you awake for the next two nights, I will change it." It did not keep me awake; I slept like a baby. This simple moment taught me to discern between what was truly important and what I needed to release.

Throughout the building process, I found myself reacting to the wolf. I worried he might show up before my house was finished. Worse, I discovered that whenever the wolf appeared, the wolf within me also emerged. Sometimes this inner wolf would tell me stories that threatened my dreams and goals. Other times, it urged me to lash out at others to satisfy its primal desires. Giving in to this wolf always created more problems.

I knew I had to stop letting the wolf control me. Instead, I had to learn to control the wolf. I resolved not to let the wolf into my house—not even while I was building it. This required confronting and working through past traumas. Losing Daddy to the wolf was the worst of these. On top of that, I had been bullied as a child by the sons of the wolf. Overcoming these experiences was essential to building the house I envisioned in my mind. I believed I could see the big picture of life, and I worked tirelessly to bring it to fruition.

My ultimate aspiration was to support others in achieving their dreams, helping them feel valued and confident on their journeys. I wanted to guide them in recognizing that the wolf exists to destroy, not to heal. I placed my trust in others and hoped they would place their trust in me. Some saw me as a people pleaser, but I considered myself a value seeker. I understood that true value in life begins with the imagination, so I encouraged others to use their creativity to build the houses of their dreams.

When I finished building my house, it was everything I had dreamed it would be: beautiful, well-constructed, and uniquely mine. It resembled a barn in some ways, and that was perfectly fine with me. My house was a reflection of my individuality, my personality, and my style.

I also expressed my uniqueness in how I dressed. I loved to dress in a way that reflects who I really am. Standing out in a crowd made me feel good, like I was letting my inner light shine for all to see. A small part of me worried that others might misunderstand, thinking I was vain or trying to be better than them. But that was never my intention. My desire was simply to be true to myself, to express what was in my heart.

And then, right on cue, the wolf arrived at my door. This time, he did not come alone—he brought his sons with him. I recognized them; I had seen them at school. Together, they launched their attack. They huffed, and they puffed…they puffed, and they huffed.

But no matter how hard they tried, they could not blow down my house.

Some might say that the wolf's sons were too young or the wolf himself was too old. The truth, however, was that my mother had learned from our family's history how to outsmart them. She had passed that wisdom on to me. As I watched the wolves slink away, tails between their legs, I heard my mother's words echo in my mind: "Do not build your house of sticks. They are not strong enough. Use lumber." Her lessons had prepared me for this moment, and they saved me.

Stick builders like me create an organized inner world within themselves. This inner world is their sanctuary, and they will fiercely defend it. To do so, they seek to control their environment, ensuring that their personal creations are safeguarded. This inner world also encompasses their reputation, another precious aspect of a stick builder's identity. Protecting their reputation is deeply tied to their sense of self-worth.

However, stick builders must be vigilant not to let the wolf in. When they attempt to impose their building model onto others, trying to control how others build their lives, problems arise. Their reputation begins to falter, conflict brews, and relationships suffer. Feathers are ruffled, friendships are strained, and resentment can grow toward the stick builder.

When this happens, the stick builder's inner world begins to collapse under the weight of their attempts to control the outer world. The balance between their internal sanctuary and external reality shifts dramatically, and not for the better. The mismanagement of their gift—their ability to organize and create—can unleash the wolf within them. What was once a harmonious inner world begins to unravel, and their reputation may come apart at the seams.

Rebuilding from this point requires great effort. If the stick builder does not act to repair the damage, their relationships may fall into disrepair entirely. And thus, the Wolf Cycle begins.

My Story as a Stick Builder

We are born as one of these builder types, as naturally ingrained in us as our fingerprints or eye color. Our builder type is not something we choose, nor can we switch to another type. However, we do have the choice to build in divine innocence, as a pig, or destroy out of ignorance, as a wolf. I was born a stick builder, and as such, I will share part of my story as the case study for this builder type.

After a long and difficult labor, Mother gave birth to me, Robert Bautner, boy number four. She was deeply disappointed that I was not a girl, but she kept me, determined to teach me as she did the rest of her children.

While I would like to say that my mother was a saint, she was not. In front of others, she was a good mother, but behind closed doors, she was a different person. In many ways, she was the wolf cloaked as an innocent pig, always playing the martyr.

I was all mixed up in my head as a child. I bore no malice toward Mother; I loved her innocently and unconditionally. Even now, I would not want it any other way. I have chosen to learn from the experiences of my upbringing. While I do not like the way I was treated, I see how I have benefited from it.

My daddy, on the other hand, was a saint. He was a kind and loving man who always brought home the bacon, ensured we had food on the table, and kept a roof over our heads. I knew without a doubt that Daddy loved me and the rest of his family. He even loved me for who I was, despite my differences from the other boys.

Mother, however, could not understand me. I did not talk until I was four and a half, and even when I did, she still could not understand me. She would often say, "I cannot understand anything you are saying. You talk in riddles!"

One thing Mother did right was to disagree with anyone who claimed there was something wrong with me. Everyone except Mother said I was retarded, but she refused to accept that. Intelligence was important to her, and she would not tolerate the idea of one of her children being anything less than intelligent. However, I cannot give her much credit for defending me. I now see that her defense was not about me but about herself. She wanted me to reflect her intelligence, to think and act like her. To her disappointment, I did not. She constantly criticized me for being different from my siblings.

The first word I ever spoke was "Googie." My brothers nicknamed me Googie after that.

Because I was not a girl, Mother devised a plan. She dressed me up as a girl, placed her curly wig on my head, and took pictures. She called me Butterball. Mother loved calling me names. My brothers laughed and teased me relentlessly. I laughed along with them, not knowing any better. I liked being the center of attention, even as the butt of their jokes. All I understood was that my antics made them happy, so I thought I should be happy too. Dressing me up as a girl temporarily satisfied Mother's longing for a daughter, but it never lasted.

Looking back, I do not think Mother ever truly liked me. She often told me she should have left me at the department store when she had the chance or drowned me in the tub. In my mind, the fact that she did not follow through with those threats meant that, deep down, she must have loved me after all. And I loved her.

Ultimately, Mother gave birth to five boys. My younger brother Walter came after me, but she never had a daughter. My older brothers were named Frank, Hermann, and Billy.

My brothers and I could not have been more different from one another. Mother knew I was the most different of all, and that was fine with me. I liked myself. I did not know any different. But Mother did not like my differences. She never understood that my uniqueness stemmed from being autistic.

Often, Mother would scream at us boys. Her yelling confused me, and because I learned differently, her frustration often led to harsh spankings. I cried all the way to my room, but she would yell after me, "Stop that crying, or I will give you something to cry about!" Knowing she was serious, I stopped.

Without a safe place in my home or the world, I found refuge inside my head. Lying on my pillow, I would bounce my head and imagine a world filled with kind people. I dreamed of becoming a millionaire, building a beautiful home, and feeling valued. My imagination became my sanctuary, and later, I worked hard to bring my dreams into the real world. I found the value of my decisions within myself before committing to them. It became vital for me to pursue purposeful dreams and desires, even as I struggled with feeling like an outcast for being different.

Mother never changed her opinion of me, but her dislike became the very thing that motivated me to succeed. I took her criticism as a challenge to prove to her and myself that my intelligence, though different, was valuable.

Being different required extra effort to navigate the world and connect with others. I taught myself by observing the world around me, particularly the behaviors of my family and those in my environment. Mother molded my brothers to be like her. They pleased her and earned her approval. To this day, they see her as a wonderful mother.

When I ventured into the world as a young man, I quickly realized that my autism had been my saving grace. At a time when no one knew how to help me, my autism kept me in a state of innocence. It shielded me from guile, anger, and malice toward my mother, brothers, and anyone else who let the wolf in them rise against me. My autism and personality gave me the courage, confidence, and self-worth to find value and trust in others.

Against all odds, I accomplished what many might call the achievements of ten lifetimes. Despite an upbringing marked by abuse and traumatic neglect, which could have left me dead, imprisoned, or addicted to drugs, I thrived.

Today, my beautiful family of five children, successful businesses, and meaningful relationships at church and with God fill me with a profound sense of self-respect and fulfillment. These achievements validate the competence and reputation I have built over the years. They are the foundation of the confidence that fuels my courage to write these books, share them with you, and speak about them to audiences across the country.

The Stick Builder Revealed

In this section, we will explore the defining traits of the stick builder. We will discuss their pursuit of beauty, their courage and confidence rooted in their inner vision, and their natural role as heroes within their communities. We will examine their deep value for control over themselves and their environment—an admirable trait that can sometimes lead others to feel controlled in their presence, though we will address this dynamic later. Stick builders are also characterized by their competitiveness, focus on reputation, and innate ability to find innovative ways to achieve their goals despite external pressures. They make unbreakable promises to themselves, valuing these commitments even more than their broader goals and dreams. While these traits are strengths, they can sometimes create friction with straw and brick builders, who may perceive stick builders as projecting an air of superiority—though this is rarely the stick builders' intent. Let us now explore these traits

"Stick builders make unbreakable promises to themselves, valuing these commitments even more than their broader goals and dreams."

more deeply, one by one.

Confidence, Courage, and Humility

Confidence is central to the stick builder's personality and is often demonstrated through their ability to keep promises to themselves and others. While confidence might seem like an essential trait for everyone, it is not equally distributed. Stick builders are naturally gifted with confidence, whereas other builder types must earn it—or, in their wolf nature, may attempt to steal it through grandstanding or intimidation. Confidence, whether innate or earned, is a powerful force, but it can also be overwhelming and costly, especially when mishandled or wielded without humility.

Courage is another hallmark of the stick builder and comes so naturally to them that it often puzzles their straw and brick counterparts. Yet even for the stick builder, courage can be a daunting force, especially when paired with humility and compassion. Courage often requires patience, as fear is a natural companion to acts of bravery. Courage and confidence work in tandem; self-control requires confidence, and confidence often hinges on the ability to summon courage. Together, these traits can mean the difference between success and failure—or even between life and death.

The distinction between confidence and courage can be likened to the difference between feeling satisfied after a meal and the hunger pangs that drive one to eat. Confidence is a sense of fulfillment, while courage is the pain of fear driving one toward action. Both are essential for overcoming challenges, and both are deeply ingrained in the stick builder's character. Unlike the other builder types, the stick builder is most likely to make unprecedented, even seemingly irrational, courageous decisions. For instance, jumping from a burning building to escape may risk life and limb, but the stick builder is more inclined to admire and emulate such acts of bravery than to hesitate in fear.

> *"Confidence is a sense of fulfillment, while courage is the pain of fear driving one toward action."*

Courage does not always manifest in life-or-death situations. It can also be seen in pursuing one's dreams, undeterred by the doubts or ridicule of others. Stick builders do not capitulate to the negativity or lack of confidence projected by others. This is where humility becomes the cornerstone of their confidence. Instead of becoming angry at those who doubt them—those who say, "You will never succeed"—stick builders use such skepticism as fuel to propel them toward their vision.

For stick builders, confidence is not arrogance; it is devotion and determination. It is the fulfillment of promises made and promises kept. It is this unwavering commitment to their inner vision that defines their unique combination of courage, confidence, and humility. It is promises made and promises kept.

Relationships, Emotions and Self-Control

The stick builder values personal freedom and individual agency above all else. While other builder types also value these principles, their perspectives differ. The stick builder naturally upholds independence as a guiding principle, whereas the brick builder must consciously choose to view independence as distinct and unique, and the straw builder must see it as separate from the system they hold dear. Speaking as a stick builder, I (Robert) see human agency as a pillar of freedom. Agency is one of God's greatest gifts to humanity.

What is agency? It is the ability to dream freely, make choices, and act upon those choices. Even a two-year-old child exercises agency when they say "no" to their parents, the very people who control their survival. Good parents redirect the child's behavior without crushing their independence. Similarly, when a two-year-old chooses to obey, they bring great joy to their parents. We are not unlike those children when it comes to God's will. God grants us agency, and our self-control is our gift back to Him. Self-control is not only a demonstration of self-respect and self-worth but also the ultimate expression of self-governance. However, self-control cannot be fully realized outside of divine innocence. By contrast, controlling others is often rooted in insecurity, pride, or poor self-esteem and reflects ignorance rather than innocence.

Human history is rife with examples of people trying to control others. This tendency has existed since the beginning of civilization.

Some individuals accept being controlled, while others resist. Unfortunately, those in positions of authority—whether as parents, community leaders, or national figures—often abuse their power. This reality is not an anomaly but an enduring pattern of human behavior.

The framers of the U.S. Constitution recognized this tendency. They sought to design a system that balanced individual freedom with communal well-being. Their goal was to prevent the strongest and most ruthless individuals from exploiting others, a phenomenon that can be observed on any schoolyard where bullies thrive. The extremes of unchecked communalism, as seen in Soviet communism, or pure individualism, as seen in ancient Greek democracy, underscore the catastrophic consequences of an imbalance in either direction.

Encouraging people to govern themselves—whether in a home, workplace, or community—generally produces positive results. History offers many examples. In early America, settlers initially embraced a socialist model where all goods were pooled into a community resource. Over time, however, it became evident that the lazy reaped the same rewards as the industrious. The system evolved to allocate land to individuals, allowing them to reap what they sowed. This shift encouraged self-governance and led to the innovation, prosperity, and work ethic that defined the nation.

I learned early in life that self-governance was critical to my future. I realized that controlling myself and my environment was essential, and I had no interest in controlling others. That would be far more work than I cared to undertake. I also learned to distinguish between those who guided me out of genuine care for my well-being and those who sought to manipulate me for their own gain.

The stick builder possesses an innate desire to control their surroundings, a gift of divine innocence that, when channeled wisely, can create a peaceful and autonomous environment for all. However, this desire can devolve into ignorance if it disregards the freedoms of others. Controlling oneself differs significantly from controlling others for personal gain. Recognizing this distinction helps us identify wolves —those who manipulate or control others for their own purposes. Some wolves use persuasive knowledge or information as a tool for self-gratification or power. Others pursue control simply to dominate.

By contrast, those who control their environment by empowering others to exercise their own autonomy foster harmony. They create spaces where control and self-control coexist without wolfish motives, allowing people to thrive in their agency and freedom. When approached with divine innocence, this balance becomes not only possible but profoundly impactful.

A good example is a farmer planting crops for human consumption. This is a good motive. The farmer can control the water through irrigation, the fertilizer, even the quality of the soil. But, ultimately the farmer cannot control the plant. He cannot control the weather, nor the sunshine nor the temperature, and yet these are all very important contributors for the plants to grow effectively or efficiently. Staying in control of the sown crop nudges the plant to produce without overt measures, but much of the process remains outside of the farmer's direct control. He can respond to varying conditions, but he cannot change them.

In my experience, the dynamic between control and agency is most intensely experienced in relationships we have with spouses, children or lifelong friends. I have also noticed throughout life that some people wear their emotions on their sleeves while others control their emotions without streaming tears. One who stays in control of the emotions may only weep (where weeping is distinct in its silent yet tearful expression of grief). Weeping is emotional but it is expressed in a controlled manner. It reminds me of the shortest verse in the Bible: "Jesus wept" (John 11:35). Jesus's weeping was a controlled and silent expression of tremendous grief. This emotional control is particularly true of the stick builder.

One interesting trait of the stick builder is that they despise the idea of community, tribe, nation, or village. For this author, a stick builder, the idea that 'it takes a village to raise a child' makes my eyes bleed. I have spoken to other stick builders who also cannot stand the words 'community' or 'tribe' or so forth. The reason for this, and the reason that it is the stick personality in particular that reacts negatively to these words and their meanings, is that the stick builder seeks self-control and control of their environment. That is impossible when control is given to this nebulous and ill-defined group called the 'community.' The stick builder intrinsically understands that putting power in the hands of the community disempowers the individual, reducing people to pawns on a chess board for whoever controls the community. It is the nightmare of the Borg in the *Star Trek* series–the hive mind that controls the individuals to such an extreme that human agency is destroyed.

Controlling one's emotions by not crying can be viewed by others as uncaring, but this is not the case. Compassion and empathy is not a product of the tears themselves or a lack of empathy. Weeping expresses emotions just as much as crying. It seems to be a part of the stick builders' method of operation. In their innocence it is a way to stay in control of themselves. This is how the stick builders often express their feelings.

The Art of the Promise

Promises are the cornerstone of the stick builder's relationship with the world. Unlike goals or commitments, which are valuable in their own right, promises hold a unique and paramount significance for the stick builder. While all three—promises, goals, and commitments—represent decisions about future actions, they differ fundamentally in how each builder type interacts with and understands them. This difference stems from the unique lens through which each builder type views the world, shaped by their divine innocence. For stick builders, promises are more than intentions—they are deeply personal bonds rooted in self-worth, integrity, and individual connection.

The Distinction Between Promises, Goals, and Commitments

Goals, the domain of the straw builder, are measurable yet flexible. They can change or evolve as new information comes to light, allowing for adaptability. Straws view life as a sort of game, with goals serving as benchmarks for measurable gains. Their focus is on winning by adhering to rules set by trusted authorities. Goals attract accountability-seekers who thrive on tangible metrics and achievements.

Brick builders, on the other hand, gravitate toward commitments. These are rooted in systems and universal principles. For bricks, commitments are firm, unwavering, and driven by a deep-seated faithfulness to their word. They see the world through the lens of systemic structures and values, often struggling to forgive failures in others' commitments, as this can challenge their sense of order and fairness.

Stick builders stand apart, seeing the world through the lens of individual connection and responsibility. Their promises, whether made to themselves, another person, or even an animal, are the strongest bonds they can create. Unlike goals, which are measurable, or commitments, which are system-oriented, promises are intensely personal. They represent a sacred determination to act with self-control, self-worth, and unwavering integrity.

Promises: A Personal Compass

For stick builders, promises are not just decisions—they are an expression of personal honor and principles. Promises embody their devotion to their own values, serving as a compass that guides their actions and reinforces their integrity. In a society that often prioritizes goal-setting as the standard for success, promises can be overlooked as a viable path to fulfilling dreams, creating personal endeavors, or achieving desires. Yet for the stick builder, promises are far more aligned with their natural way of being.

Unlike goals, which can feel tied to external regimens or rules imposed by authority figures, promises are inherently free of authoritarian constraints. Stick builders often view regimens as tools of control that restrict individual freedom. This perspective extends to systems and authority structures, such as governments or organizations, which they believe frequently fail to serve the individual's best interests. Instead, promises empower the stick builder to pursue their aspirations on their own terms, guided by their unique principles and values.

The Limitations of Goals and Commitments for Stick Builders

To stick builders, both goals and commitments present challenges that conflict with their divine innocence. Goals, with their reliance on measurable outcomes and rules, can feel impersonal and disconnected from the stick builder's inner vision. Similarly, commitments, while admirable for their steadfastness, are often too tied to systems, making them feel restrictive or overly institutional.

Stick builders, who value personal freedom and agency above all else, are acutely aware of the limitations inherent in these approaches. They recognize that systems and rules, though created with good intentions, often stray far from their original purpose. Instead of improving life for individuals, they can become mechanisms of control that strip people of their autonomy. This disconnect makes goal-setting and system-based commitments inherently unappealing to the stick builder.

The Power of Promises

By contrast, promises represent the ultimate expression of the stick builder's divine innocence. Promises are personal, flexible, and rooted in the stick builder's integrity. They are experienced as a determination to act in alignment with one's principles and values, regardless of external pressures. Through promises, stick builders substantiate their commitment to themselves and their unique purpose in the world.

When a stick builder makes a promise, they tap into their inner strength, self-control, and courage to overcome obstacles and resistance. Their promises are not about conforming to societal expectations or adhering to arbitrary rules. Instead, they are about honoring the deeply personal bond they have with their own integrity. This makes promises a powerful tool for stick builders to achieve their dreams, create meaningful endeavors, and live authentically.

Promises and Divine Innocence

For the stick builder, promises are not just about achieving outcomes —they are about staying true to one's divine innocence. They embody the stick builder's commitment to live with integrity, courage, and self-respect. By honoring their promises, stick builders not only fulfill their personal aspirations but also inspire others to do the same.

In a world that often emphasizes goals and commitments, the stick builder's reliance on promises offers a refreshing perspective. It reminds us that success is not just about measurable achievements or adherence to systems—it is about staying true to oneself, honoring one's values, and building a life that reflects one's unique purpose. For the stick builder, this is the art of the promise: a deeply personal, transformative path to living with meaning and authenticity.

Feeling Like a Misfit and Using That Feeling to Beat the System

The beauty of an allegory lies in its ability to reveal truths about the human mind. Rudolph the Red-Nosed Reindeer serves as a perfect allegory for the stick builder, and we would venture to guess that many stick builders are drawn to this Christmas classic. Rudolph was born with a unique gift that made him shine, yet he was ridiculed for being different. Deep within every stick builder lies a similar story. This experience of feeling different is distinct to the stick builder and is tied to their "shine," their inner light, and even their sparkle.

Stick builders love to shine. They thrive in the spotlight, which gives them a sense of value and purpose. Some use the spotlight for good, operating within their divine innocence. Others, however, can become so enamored with the attention that it turns into an addiction, and they pursue it at any cost. When this happens, they fall out of divine innocence and into their wolfish, ignorant nature.

Regardless of how they handle their shine, there are times when stick builders feel unappreciated or undervalued. Even in these moments, they instinctively know they are an asset, even when society sees them as a liability. Rudolph faced this exact challenge. He was rejected for being different and labeled a misfit, but the very trait that made him stand out—his glowing nose—ultimately saved Christmas. By the end of the story, Rudolph's unique gift was celebrated, and he was honored by leading Santa's sleigh.

This theme resonates with me (Robert) personally, as it reminds me of my father's story. My father was a misfit in his native Germany, and when asked why he left, he would always say, "I did not want to surrender myself to someone else's ambitions." Born in 1913, just before World War I, my father grew up amidst destruction and economic devastation. By age 25, as Germany stood on the brink of another war, he faced the prospect of being drafted into Hitler's army.

At first, my father complied. He was trained, uniformed, and sent to Austria in 1938. While there was no resistance, the anguish he witnessed stayed with him. Upon returning home, he saw Hitler's followers celebrating and preparing for further conquests. It was then that he decided he would not surrender his future to someone else's ambitions. This choice made him a misfit, but he stood firm, refusing to become a pawn in Hitler's insatiable quest for power. Through determination and courage, my father found a legal way to escape to America, ultimately becoming a citizen. This decision not only saved his life but also made it possible for my four brothers and me to be born in America. I will always be grateful for his decision to stand against the system.

The Danger of Surrendering Your Future
Surrendering your future to someone else's ambitions is a common, yet often unnoticed, phenomenon. Even in America, where freedom is celebrated, many individuals unknowingly align their futures with the

ambitions of others. A simple example is the corporate workspace. For some, the structure of a cubicle-based job is a good fit. They adapt to the environment and, while they may occasionally complain, they find satisfaction in their work. These individuals willingly and innocently align their futures with their company's goals.

However, for others, such an environment is stifling. It feels soul-sucking and even violates their divine innocence. These individuals are the misfits, those who cannot fit into the system. For them, surrendering to the system is a betrayal of their true selves.

Stick builders often find themselves in this category. When they are reduced to a cog in a machine, they feel restless and disconnected. This sense of self-betrayal compels them to act. They rebel against rules and systems that limit their individuality, rejecting expectations of obedience. They see through the façade of education and social structures designed to make everyone conform. Those who resist these systems are often labeled failures by the rulemakers.

For stick builders, surrendering control of their independence and values leads to personal demise. Their divine innocence drives them to either fight the system or abandon it altogether to create a world where they can thrive.

Beating the System

When stick builders choose to step away from the system, they carve out a parallel world for themselves. They continue to live within society but create a personal domain where their values and principles take precedence. This approach, which I call "beating the world at its own game," allows them to preserve their divine innocence and maintain their autonomy.

For stick builders, this is not just about survival—it is about thriving in a way that aligns with their true selves. By prioritizing prudence, self-control, and respect for others, they create a personal world that limits their participation in the larger system.

Rudolph as a Model for Stick Builders

Rudolph's story perfectly illustrates the journey of a stick builder. When his father tried to make him fit in by covering his nose, the effort failed. Rudolph, feeling rejected, ran away. By withdrawing from the system, he defeated its control over him. He created a new life for himself with other misfits, a life that honored his individuality.

Even so, Rudolph still loved his home. He wanted to use his gifts to help his people but knew he could not betray himself to do so. When Santa finally gave him the opportunity to shine, Rudolph not only saved Christmas but also created a new system that included all the misfits, even the once-feared Bumble.

This outcome is the ideal for the stick builder: to shine, share their gifts, and save the world while making it better for everyone. It is a testament to the power of divine innocence, resilience, and the courage to stand apart in a world that often demands conformity.

Roles of The Innocent Stick Builder

Magnet to Personal Success

Every builder type strives for success, but their definitions of success differ. While all builders value recognition, they seek it in unique ways. For the stick builder, success is deeply personal and non-negotiable. Where the brick builder finds success in their impact and the straw builder in their experiences, the stick builder's success revolves around beauty, individuality, and inspiring others to reach their fullest potential.

Stick builders are naturally inclined to focus on personal achievements and the success of those around them. They view their individual triumphs as a reflection of their unique identity and their ability to overcome challenges. For instance, I (Robert) once stayed up all night thinking about a sickly horse brought to my farm. My mental focus was on how I could help the horse look as it should—healthy, vibrant, and beautiful. A brick builder might have prioritized the horse's overall health, and a straw builder might have been concerned with its immediate experience. Stick builders, however, are driven by a vision of beauty and potential.

This drive to stand out is also why stick builders are often drawn to roles where they can shine—whether as celebrities, lead musicians, or influential speakers. They tend to dress boldly and uniquely, expressing their individuality in every facet of their lives. For them, success is not just a goal; it is a personal challenge. They thrive on encouraging others to achieve their own personal successes while holding themselves to high standards of self-recognition.

Transformer of Negatives into Positives

Stick builders possess a remarkable ability to find value in the negative events of life. Childhood traumas, bullying, or favoritism within families often serve as fuel for their dreams rather than deterrents. For instance, a stick builder who was told they were worthless by a playground bully might make a promise to themselves to prove the bully wrong. When they remain in divine innocence, stick builders consistently turn hardships into stepping stones toward personal achievement.

Few people grow up in entirely positive environments, and those who do often struggle when faced with the harsh realities of life. Stick builders, however, have an advantage. Unlike brick builders, who must fully process negative events to overcome them, or straw builders, who often reject the idea that negatives can be transformed into positives, stick builders naturally understand that positivity and negativity are subjective. If they cannot immediately see the positive within a negative, they work to create it.

Stick builders recognize that positivity can heal the mind, body, and soul, but they also understand that positivity alone is insufficient. Ignoring life's negatives or dismissing them as irrelevant creates fertile ground for disappointment, despair, and feelings of failure. Stick builders embrace the struggle, using setbacks as opportunities to try harder, adapt, or change tactics. They understand that success requires the balance of positives and negatives, much like a battery needs both poles to generate power.

This perspective is a valuable lesson for all builder types. Negativity is not inherently evil or indicative of failure. Instead, it is an energy source that, when acknowledged and harnessed, can fuel growth and transformation.

Transformer of Trauma into Art

One of the most profound ways stick builders turn negatives into positives is by creating art from trauma. While not all stick builders are traditional artists, many view success itself as a form of art. For them, art is a transmutation of pain into beauty, joy, and fulfillment.

Art can take many forms: dance, drama, painting, literature, music, poetry, or even financial success. For instance, a stick builder might channel their energy into building a business, founding a nonprofit, or creating a successful investment portfolio. These achievements are as much artistic expressions as a painter's masterpiece or a poet's verse.

When stick builders refuse to give up, no matter the obstacles, they transform their lives into works of art. This transformation is deeply personal. No other builder type is as invested in their individuality, creations, or vision of the world as the stick builder.

Some of the most influential artists draw inspiration from deep-rooted pain. For others, healing comes through analyzing and processing trauma. But suppressing pain or masking it with superficial positivity is always a mistake. To deny one's pain is to deny one's art. Suppressed pain will only lead to more suffering.

The artist, by contrast, turns their pain—whether from abuse, physical injury, illness, or a toxic relationship—into empowerment. Seeking transformation is an exhilarating act that can lead to personal breakthroughs and profound creations. By expressing pain, stick builders find freedom and the ability to create beauty from ashes.

A Creative Drive Fueled by the Inner Self

For stick builders, the journey from pain to promise to creation completes the circuit of self-expression. Their art, whether literal or metaphorical, is the release of trapped pain and the realization of their unique gifts. They understand that their art—be it a painting, a business, or a compassionate act—has the power to change lives, save the world, and uplift the human spirit.

"By expressing pain, stick builders find freedom and the ability to create beauty from ashes."

This is human empowerment at its finest. By transforming their trauma into art, stick builders create a legacy of resilience and beauty. They stand as living testaments to the power of divine innocence and the profound strength that comes from embracing both life's positives and negatives.

A Dreamer Who Wants to Save the World

The stick builder sees himself as a hero, someone who saves the world from evil, from danger, from its own demise. Stick builder heroes succeed through grit and personal energy and action. As an example, this author is a stick builder, and it has been my stated intention to save civilization through the ideas in this book. Superman, Spiderman, and Wonder Woman used their might, their power and abilities, to save civilization. These heroes can be differentiated from Iron Man who was a straw personality. He was intrigued with his technologies and what he created. He was an accidental hero, in a sense. So was Batman. It could be argued Batman was a brick personality who rescued Gotham City.

There is a vast difference between saving the world and rescuing the world. It is primarily a matter of perception, yet it is critical. When the stick builder decides to save the world in their divine innocence, they are viewing the world as a population of individuals with hopes, dreams, ambitions, and value. The world to them is not a singular, nebulous entity. It is individuals, all of whom are equals to the stick builder who desires to save them. To rescue the world is quite the opposite in that rescuing implies superiority to the individual who is being helped. To the rescuer, the individual being helped is perceived as weaker because of the state they are in.

The Stick Builder in the State of Ignorance

When Divine Innocence Falls to Ignorance

When the stick builder departs from their divine innocence, their gifts of confidence, creativity, and influence become distorted. Instead of serving as tools for inspiration and leadership, these qualities morph into mechanisms of manipulation and control. The stick builder in ignorance often falls into two destructive archetypes: the drama queen, who seeks constant attention and validation, and the martyr, who weaponizes their sacrifices to control others.

The Drama Queen

In the state of ignorance, the stick builder's desire to shine and stand out warps into a need for excessive attention, often at the expense of others. When wronged—or even when perceiving a slight—they react not with measured confidence but with explosive dramatics. They are the ones who gather their friends into a frenzy, turning them against the perceived offender, ensuring that the narrative casts them as the victim and hero simultaneously.

Their tools are emotional manipulation and gossip. They thrive on retelling stories of how they were wronged, each retelling more dramatic than the last, designed to captivate their audience and solidify their position as the center of attention. They burst into tears at will, not out of genuine emotion but to elicit sympathy and reinforce their control over others. Their volume increases as they dominate conversations, ensuring all eyes remain on them.

Rather than encouraging others to shine alongside them, they hoard the spotlight, claiming it as their exclusive domain. Their charisma, which in innocence could inspire and unite, now isolates and divides as they pit people against each other, all in service of their own ego. To them, relationships are a means to an end, and that end is to maximize their own attention and validation.

The Classic Narcissist

The classic narcissist is an extreme manifestation of the stick builder in ignorance. Their confidence has spiraled into arrogance, and their courage has been replaced with an insatiable hunger for power and control. Historical figures like Adolf Hitler embody this archetype: a stick builder who used their natural charisma, vision, and determination to manipulate and dominate rather than inspire and uplift.

The narcissistic stick builder craves admiration and will go to any lengths to achieve it, even if it means harming others or dismantling systems. They see themselves as superior to those around them, using their influence to build not a house but an empire, one designed to serve their ego and reinforce their perceived greatness. Their ability to inspire and lead is used not for collective good but for personal gain, with no regard for the destruction left in their wake.

These individuals manipulate those around them like pawns, positioning people to serve their needs and discarding them when they are no longer useful. Their natural competitiveness turns into ruthless ambition, and their focus on reputation becomes an obsession with power. They are skilled at using charm and deception to achieve their goals, masking their wolfish nature behind a façade of strength and confidence.

The Key Difference: Divine Innocence vs. Ignorance

The stick builder's innate gifts of creativity, courage, and influence are powerful tools, but when these tools are wielded in ignorance, they create destruction rather than beauty. Instead of inspiring others to reach their potential, the stick builder in ignorance uses others as stepping stones to their own ends. Instead of building a house of strength and character, they build a fragile façade, one that crumbles under the weight of their self-serving motives.

The stick builder in divine innocence stands out because they create beauty and inspire greatness in others, but the stick builder in ignorance stands apart for the damage they cause in their pursuit of attention and control. The journey back to divine innocence requires them to recognize their wolfish tendencies, confront their insecurities, and embrace their true purpose: to build a life of value, not vanity, and to shine in a way that brings light to others, not just themselves.

The Stick Builder as a Martyr in the State of Ignorance

When the stick builder succumbs to ignorance, their natural courage, resilience, and sense of personal responsibility can devolve into a distorted martyr complex. Instead of using their gifts to inspire others and build a strong, independent foundation, the stick builder as a martyr turns their struggles into a stage for self-pity and manipulation. They wield their sacrifices not as acts of love or service but as weapons to control those around them, feeding their wolfish need for recognition and validation.

The Martyr's Cry: "Look at All I Have Done for You"

In their divine innocence, the stick builder values promises and integrity, often going to great lengths to fulfill their commitments. However, in ignorance, these promises become a tool for self-aggrandizement. The stick builder as a martyr constantly reminds others of the sacrifices they have made, emphasizing their suffering to elicit guilt or admiration. Every act of service or generosity is recounted in painstaking detail, ensuring that no one forgets the "burden" they have shouldered.

Their martyrdom is not rooted in genuine selflessness but in a desire to maintain control. By framing themselves as the long-suffering victim who has "done it all," they subtly (or overtly) demand loyalty, gratitude, and obedience from those they claim to serve. Their suffering becomes a currency, exchanged for influence and power over others.

Weaponizing Sacrifice

The martyr stick builder often uses their perceived sacrifices to manipulate those around them. They frame their actions as noble and selfless, while quietly resenting the lack of recognition they feel they deserve. This resentment fuels their wolfish tendencies, leading them to passive-aggressively punish others for not adequately acknowledging their efforts.

For example, they might say, "After everything I have done for you, this is how you repay me?" or "If it weren't for me, where would you be?" These statements are designed to instill guilt and reinforce their role as the "savior" in the relationship. Their sacrifices, once an expression of love and integrity, become a means of controlling others and maintaining their own sense of superiority.

The Martyr's Isolation

Ironically, the stick builder as a martyr often isolates themselves through their wolfish behavior. Their constant focus on their own struggles and sacrifices alienates those around them, who may feel overwhelmed, manipulated, or unappreciated. Instead of fostering connection and mutual respect, the martyr's behavior creates a barrier, leaving them feeling lonely and unfulfilled.

This isolation feeds the martyr's narrative of victimhood, reinforcing their belief that they are unappreciated and misunderstood. The cycle continues as they double down on their sacrifices, hoping to gain the recognition and connection they crave, but driving others further away in the process.

The Key Difference: Divine Sacrifice vs. Wolfish Martyrdom

In divine innocence, the stick builder's sacrifices are acts of love, integrity, and purpose. They give freely, without expecting anything in return, and their actions inspire others to do the same. In ignorance, however, their sacrifices become transactional. They give not out of love but out of a need for control, validation, and recognition.

The stick builder as a martyr must confront their wolfish tendencies to reclaim their divine innocence. This requires them to let go of their need for external validation and focus instead on the intrinsic value of their actions. When they do so, their sacrifices become genuine expressions of love and strength, rather than tools for manipulation and control.

By stepping back into their divine innocence, the stick builder can transform their wolfish martyrdom into a source of true connection and inspiration. They can build relationships rooted in mutual respect and support, using their natural gifts to uplift others rather than to dominate or control. In doing so, they reclaim their role as a hero, not through suffering but through strength and grace.

Returning to Innocence: The Journey Back

The journey of returning to innocence for the stick builder is one of profound self-reflection, healing, and transformation. It requires the stick builder to confront the wolfish tendencies that have overtaken them, acknowledge their impact on others and themselves, and make conscious choices to re-center their lives in divine innocence. While this process can be challenging, it is deeply rewarding, as it allows the stick builder to reclaim their true nature as a builder of beauty, integrity, and connection.

Acknowledging the Wolf Within

The first step in returning to innocence is recognizing the wolfish behaviors that have taken hold. For the stick builder, this often means acknowledging patterns of control, manipulation, or martyrdom. These tendencies may have developed as coping mechanisms in response to pain, fear, or unmet needs, but they have led the stick builder away from their true nature.

Self-awareness is key. The stick builder must examine their thoughts, actions, and motives honestly. They must ask themselves difficult questions:

- Am I using my sacrifices to manipulate others?
- Am I trying to control people or situations to feel secure?

- Am I seeking validation or attention through my struggles?
- Have I placed my sense of worth in the hands of others rather than within myself?

By answering these questions with humility and courage, the stick builder begins to see where they have departed from their divine innocence. This self-awareness is not about self-condemnation but about taking responsibility and making the choice to change.

Letting Go of Control

The stick builder's desire for control, when guided by divine innocence, is a gift that allows them to create order, beauty, and stability. However, in a state of ignorance, this desire becomes a need to dominate, micromanage, or manipulate. To return to innocence, the stick builder must learn to release their grip on control, particularly over others.

This requires a shift in focus:

- Instead of trying to control others, the stick builder must prioritize self-control.
- Instead of manipulating situations to achieve a specific outcome, they must trust in the natural flow of life and the agency of others.
- Instead of viewing others as extensions of their plans, they must see them as individuals with their own paths and purposes.

Letting go of control does not mean becoming passive or

disengaged. Rather, it means embracing a mindset of collaboration and trust. The stick builder learns to guide and inspire rather than impose and demand. They rediscover the joy of working with others as equals, valuing their contributions and respecting their autonomy.

Reframing Sacrifice

For the stick builder, sacrifice is a natural expression of their integrity and love. In divine innocence, sacrifice is given freely, without expectation of recognition or reward. However, in a state of ignorance, sacrifice becomes transactional—a means to gain validation, loyalty, or compliance.

To return to innocence, the stick builder must reframe their understanding of sacrifice. They must learn to give from a place of abundance rather than lack, recognizing that their worth is not determined by how much they sacrifice but by the love and integrity they bring to their actions.

This involves:

- Setting healthy boundaries to avoid overextending themselves.
- Practicing self-care to replenish their energy and maintain balance.
- Giving without attachment to the outcome, trusting that their efforts have value regardless of how they are received.

When the stick builder approaches sacrifice from a place of divine innocence, it becomes a source of joy and connection rather than a burden or a weapon. It strengthens their relationships and reinforces their sense of purpose.

Embracing Humility and Vulnerability

Returning to innocence requires the stick builder to embrace both humility and vulnerability. In their wolfish state, they may use confidence as a shield to conceal their fears or weaknesses, resisting the admission of mistakes or the act of seeking help out of fear that it will lower their perceived value. For example, stick builders in their divine innocence are not naturally quick-witted like their brick and straw counterparts. This can leave them feeling vulnerable or inferior in situations where quick responses are valued or when others excel at providing them.

If the stick builder succumbs to the wolf in these moments, they may become manipulative or combative as a means of compensating for their discomfort. To remain in their divine innocence, the stick builder must humbly accept that quick thinking is not their strength and resist the urge to compete with those for whom it is. Instead, they can recognize that they are not meant to excel in all things and that their unique strengths bring their own value. Even when others expect quick responses, the stick builder can stay true to their divine innocence by calmly explaining that they need time to reflect before offering an answer. This honest approach not only preserves their authenticity but also fosters respect and understanding in their relationships.

In divine innocence, humility is a profound strength. When the stick builder embraces humility and vulnerability, they begin to dismantle the walls that ignorance has built around their heart. This openness allows them to receive love, support, and understanding, fostering a deep sense of belonging and mutual respect. By acknowledging their imperfections, the stick builder creates space to learn from their experiences and build authentic connections with others. Vulnerability becomes a powerful bridge to deeper relationships, inviting others to see and cherish the stick builder for who they truly are—gifts, gaps, and all.

Transforming Pain into Purpose

A defining trait of the stick builder is their ability to transform negatives into positives. This gift is especially important in the journey back to innocence. The stick builder must confront the pain, trauma, or unmet needs that contributed to their wolfish behaviors and find a way to turn them into sources of growth and inspiration.

This process involves:

- Acknowledging and processing their pain, rather than suppressing or ignoring it.
- Seeking meaning in their experiences, asking, "What can I learn from this? How can this make me stronger or wiser?"
- Channeling their pain into creative expression, whether through

art, writing, music, or other forms of personal fulfillment.

By transforming pain into purpose, the stick builder not only heals themselves but also inspires others. Their journey becomes a testament to the resilience of the human spirit and the power of divine innocence.

Rebuilding Relationships

As the stick builder returns to innocence, they may need to rebuild relationships that were damaged by their wolfish behaviors. This requires humility, accountability, and a commitment to change. The stick builder must:

- Apologize sincerely for any harm they caused, without justifying or minimizing their actions.
- Show through their actions that they are committed to growth and transformation.
- Reestablish trust by being consistent, reliable, and respectful in their interactions.

Rebuilding relationships is not always easy, and not every relationship can or should be repaired. However, the stick builder's commitment to living in divine innocence will naturally attract people who value and support their journey.

Reclaiming Their Role as a Hero

In their divine innocence, the stick builder is a natural hero, using their courage, confidence, and creativity to inspire and uplift others.

Returning to innocence allows them to reclaim this role, not as a martyr or a manipulator but as a genuine source of light and hope.

The stick builder rediscovers their ability to lead by example, to create beauty and meaning in the world, and to empower others to do the same. They become a builder not just of structures or systems but of lives, helping others see their own potential and achieve their own dreams.

The Ultimate Gift of Returning to Innocence

When the stick builder returns to innocence, they reconnect with the truth of who they are: a creator, a dreamer, and a force for good in the world. They let go of the need for validation or control and embrace the freedom of living authentically.

In doing so, they not only transform their own lives but also inspire others to find their own paths to divine innocence. The stick builder becomes a beacon of hope, demonstrating that no matter how far we may stray into ignorance, the journey back to innocence is always possible—and always worth it.

The Stick Builder's Connection to Jesus and His Riddles

The stick builder expresses the whisperings of the universe in language that preserves its mysteries. For this reason, they are sometimes accused of speaking in riddles. Jesus often communicated in the same way. At times, His meaning was clear, but other times, He left His listeners with more questions than answers. His use of parables is a prime example—each story carried a deeper truth hidden beneath the surface. Even His disciples were perplexed by this and once asked, "Why do You speak to them in parables?" In true stick-builder fashion, Jesus answered with yet another mystery: "Because it has been given to you to know the mysteries of the kingdom of heaven, but to them it has not been given." His response was layered with meaning, requiring deeper contemplation rather than offering a direct explanation.

Stick builders instinctively understand this approach. They relate to Jesus's way of speaking, recognizing that the mysteries of creation cannot be reduced to simple explanations. To do so would diminish their depth and significance. In their divine innocence, they perceive the infinite, expansive truth of God and seek to honor it in the way they communicate. Whereas the straw builder seeks information and clarity, and the brick builder pursues harmony and order, the stick builder embraces the mystery. They have the confidence and courage to immerse themselves in the unknown, navigating uncertainty with an unwavering commitment to truth. Even when faced with danger or doubt, they remain steadfast, knowing that the journey itself is an expression of their spiritual connection.

The Cryptic and Sometimes Outrageous Voice of the Stick

Thus, the stick builder connects to the Person of Jesus. This connection is more than symbolic. Jesus, a carpenter by trade, embodies the essence of the stick—a savior, teacher, and servant leader. It is no coincidence that the stick builder's qualities and voice reflect these aspects of Christ.

Like the straw, the stick builder is endowed with God's attributes, including love, compassion, forgiveness, mercy, grace, truth, wisdom, power, holiness, faithfulness, and goodness. Yet the stick's unique divine connection manifests in their focus on saving others from the wolves of the world. This aligns with Jesus's role as the Light of the World, both fully divine and fully human, embodying the ultimate savior and servant. Stick builders, like Jesus, are willing to sacrifice their own needs and comforts to protect, heal, and guide others.

Unlike the straw's calming voice, the stick builder's voice carries strength and authority. In Revelation, Jesus's voice is described as "like the sound of many waters" (Revelation 1:15). Water, with its rushing, roaring, and unrelenting power, is an apt metaphor for the commanding nature of Jesus's voice—and that of the stick builder. The Bible also highlights the powerful projection of Jesus's voice in pivotal moments. On the cross, Jesus cried out in a loud voice, "Eli, Eli, lama sabachthani?" (Matthew 27:46), and later, with a final loud cry, He gave up His spirit (Matthew 27:50). His voice was not soft or subdued; it carried conviction and clarity. Stick builders, similarly, have a voice that is confident and commanding. Their speech is not merely loud but carries an undeniable authority. They are unafraid to express themselves powerfully, and when they speak, people listen—even if they do not always understand.

Stick builders also share Jesus's tendency to speak in ways that seem cryptic or enigmatic. Their statements can feel like riddles, leaving listeners puzzled or even frustrated. My own mother often told me to stop "talking in riddles" because she found my communication style hard to follow. Jesus faced similar misunderstandings. He often answered questions with more questions or gave answers that seemed deliberately mysterious. For example, when Pontius Pilate asked if He was the King of the Jews, Jesus responded with, "Is that your own idea, or did others talk to you about me?" (John 18:33-34). Earlier that day, when asked by the high priest if He was the Christ, Jesus affirmed, "I am," but followed it with the enigmatic statement, "And you will see the Son of Man sitting at the right hand of the Mighty One and coming on the clouds of heaven" (Mark 14:61-62). This tendency to speak cryptically often left people confused, but Jesus remained unbothered by their misunderstanding. Similarly, stick builders are content to let others figure out their meaning, confident that they have been clear enough.

Another example of the stick builder's bold communication style is Jesus's sermon after feeding the multitude. Knowing that many followed Him only for the free food, Jesus shocked them with an outrageous statement: "Unless you eat the flesh of the Son of Man and drink His blood, you have no life in you" (John 6:53). Without the perspective of modern Christianity, this was a bizarre and unsettling statement. Even many of His disciples left after hearing it, unable to grasp His meaning. When Jesus asked the Twelve if they, too, would leave, Peter—a classic stick builder—replied, "Lord, to whom shall we go? You have the words of eternal life" (John 6:68). Like Jesus and Peter, stick builders are known for making statements that can seem shocking or offensive to those who do not understand their deeper meaning.

Stick builders are natural heroes, driven by a deep desire to save and protect others, even at great personal cost. This reflects Jesus's courage and compassion in defending the weak and marginalized. He stood up for the woman caught in adultery, healed the sick and demon-possessed, and welcomed children when others dismissed them. Jesus valued the downtrodden, saying, "The kingdom of God belongs to such as these" (Luke 18:16). Similarly, stick builders are not afraid to champion the causes of those who are overlooked or oppressed. They will stand against societal norms, risking ridicule or rejection, to do what is right. This heroism can make them appear dramatic or even reckless to brick builders, who value stability, and irritating to straw builders, who prefer subtlety. Yet stick builders are undeterred by such perceptions, remaining steadfast in their mission to bring healing and hope to others.

The stick builder's voice is a powerful reflection of their divine connection to Jesus. It is loud, commanding, and at times cryptic or outrageous, but it carries a purpose: to challenge, to heal, and to save. Stick builders, like Jesus, are unafraid to speak the truth boldly, even when it is misunderstood or rejected. Their heroism and willingness to sacrifice for others make them invaluable in the fight against the wolves of the world. When rooted in divine innocence, the stick builder's voice becomes a beacon of hope, courage, and transformation.

In the next section, you will have the opportunity to take a quiz to determine if you are a stick builder. This quiz is designed to separate the stick builder from other types by honing in on the core traits of the stick. There is one caveat to this: it is possible to score as a stick builder when one is actually another type if one is living inauthentically. This can happen when a person has been raised by a stick builder, particularly a narcissistic one, that has led one to believe that stick builder traits are the best or, worse, are the only good way to live. Of course, this can be the case for any builder type. If you do find that you are outside of your divine innocence, there is no shame or guilt in this. There is simply the need to act–to move toward innocence and discover your true self. It is time to return to the home of your soul, knowing you are safe from the wolf.

How can one possibly know whether you are exhibiting the

behaviors of your true builder type? One significant sign that you are living inauthentically as a stick builder is that you feel drained and disconnected from others and even yourself. This means you are outside of your divine innocence. If you suspect that you might be living outside of your innocence, take time to study and contemplate the traits of all three builder types, and then observe yourself in relationships with others. Ask yourself, when do I feel fulfilled, natural, and empowered? It was through the combination of study and observation of myself and others that I (Robert) learned that I was a stick builder who had been mimicking the traits of a brick because of my domineering mother. It was through this process that I returned to divine innocence and to my true builder type. In sum, being in divine innocence means correctly identifying and living in one's true type. With this in mind, proceed to the quiz. You will be able to score it at the end.

QUIZ

ARE YOU A STICK BUILDER?

In this section, you will have the opportunity to take a quiz to determine if you are a stick builder. This quiz is designed to separate the stick builder from other types by honing in on the core traits of the stick. There is one caveat to this: it is possible to score as a stick builder when one is actually another type if one is living inauthentically. This can happen when a person has been raised by a stick builder, particularly a narcissistic one, that has led one to believe that stick builder traits are the best or, worse, are the only good way to live. Of course, this can be the case for any builder type. If you do find that you are outside of your divine innocence, there is no shame or guilt in this. There is simply the need to act–to move toward innocence and discover your true self. It is time to return to the home of your soul, knowing you are safe from the wolf.

How can one possibly know whether you are exhibiting the behaviors of your true builder type? One significant sign that you are living inauthentically as a stick builder is that you feel drained and disconnected from others and even yourself. This means you are outside of your divine innocence. If you suspect that you might be living outside of your innocence, take time to study and contemplate the traits of all three builder types, and then observe yourself in relationships with others. Ask yourself, when do I feel fulfilled, natural, and empowered? It was through the combination of study and observation of myself and others that I myself learned that I was a stick builder who had been mimicking the traits of a brick because of my domineering mother. It was through this process that I returned to divine innocence and to my true builder type. In sum, being in divine innocence means correctly identifying and living in one's true type. With this in mind, proceed to the quiz. You will be able to score it at the end.

Reflect on each of the questions below, and answer each using the following scale:

1 Never

2 Rarely

3 Sometimes

4 Often

5 Always

1. Do you value beauty and strive to incorporate it into every aspect of your life?

   1 - 2 - 3 - 4 - 5

2. Do you prioritize protecting your reputation?

   1 - 2 - 3 - 4 - 5

3. Is dressing authentically, according to your personal style, for every occasion important to you?

   1 - 2 - 3 - 4 - 5

4. Do you like to stay in control of your environment?

   1 - 2 - 3 - 4 - 5

5. Do you consider recognizing the value in others one of your highest priorities?

   1 - 2 - 3 - 4 - 5

6. Do you manage your environment to enhance your value or the value of your work?

   1 - 2 - 3 - 4 - 5

7. Do you demonstrate courage and confidence by staying focused on a vision you have developed in your inner world?

   1 - 2 - 3 - 4 - 5

8. Do you find innovative ways to achieve your goals, even if they challenge existing rules or expectations?

   1 - 2 - 3 - 4 - 5

9. Do you actively seek value in experiences that most people dismiss as negative, such as trauma or hardship?

   1 - 2 - 3 - 4 - 5

10. Do you enjoy sharing insights about what is happening in the world and why it matters?

    1 - 2 - 3 - 4 - 5

11. If you had to relate to God the Father, Son, or Holy Spirit, would you choose the Son?

    1 - 2 - 3 - 4 - 5

12. Do you feel the need for validation in your relationships to feel secure?

    1 - 2 - 3 - 4 - 5

13. Do you view money as a means of expressing yourself?

    1 - 2 - 3 - 4 - 5

14. Do you struggle to be quick-witted?

    1 - 2 - 3 - 4 - 5

15. Are you motivated to prove people wrong when they criticize or doubt you?

    1 - 2 - 3 - 4 - 5

16. When you meet someone, do you have a tendency to test their character by asking them direct questions?

    1 - 2 - 3 - 4 - 5

17. Do you respond best to bold, cryptic language?

    1 - 2 - 3 - 4 - 5

18. Do you seldom if ever cry over sad or emotional stories?

    1 - 2 - 3 - 4 - 5

19. Do others accuse you of speaking in riddles or nonsensical language?

    1 - 2 - 3 - 4 - 5

20. Do you relate to making promises with others more than setting goals?

    1 - 2 - 3 - 4 - 5

21. Do you like to stay in control of your environment?

1 - 2 - 3 - 4 - 5

22. Do you tend to give long, drawn-out answers when someone asks you a question?

1 - 2 - 3 - 4 - 5

How to Score Your Quiz:

If your score is between 88-110 you are most likely a stick builder living in your divine innocence. If your score was less than 88, you are most likely a different builder type.

Are You a Stick Builder Living as the Wolf?

If your score indicates that you are a stick builder, take this quiz to determine the extent to which you are either living in innocence as the pig or ignorance as the wolf. If you are certain that you are a different type, skip this quiz and go to the next chapter.

Reflect on each of the questions below, and answer each using the following scale:

1 Never

2 Rarely

3 Sometimes

4 Often

5 Always

1. Do you feel the need to dominate conversations to ensure all attention is focused on you?

   1 - 2 - 3 - 4 - 5

2. Do you tend to exaggerate situations to gain sympathy or attention from others?

   1 - 2 - 3 - 4 - 5

3. Have you ever used emotional outbursts, such as crying or anger, to manipulate others into giving you what you want?

   1 - 2 - 3 - 4 - 5

4. Do you often find yourself gossiping about others to rally people to your side in a conflict?

   1 - 2 - 3 - 4 - 5

5. Do you feel uneasy or unimportant when you are not the center of attention in a group?

   1 - 2 - 3 - 4 - 5

6. Do you frequently make promises to others that you struggle to keep or only make to gain favor in the moment?

   1 - 2 - 3 - 4 - 5

7. Do you sometimes find yourself valuing the spotlight or recognition over genuine connections with others?

   1 - 2 - 3 - 4 - 5

8. Have people ever told you that you manipulate situations to suit your needs or desires?

   1 - 2 - 3 - 4 - 5

9. Do you find yourself overly focused on how others perceive you, sometimes at the expense of authenticity?

   1 - 2 - 3 - 4 - 5

10. Do you feel resentful or competitive when others receive attention, recognition, or praise that you believe should have been yours?

    1 - 2 - 3 - 4 - 5

11. When you are against someone, do you trick them to watch them fail?

    1 - 2 - 3 - 4 - 5

How to Score the Quiz:

The Wolf: A score between 44-55 indicates more wolf-like tendencies and ignorance of your actions. You are most certainly living as the wolf if you scored in this range.

The Pig: A score between 22-43 indicates that you are living in divine innocence most of the time. Your lower score shows that you have greater awareness and commitment to living in innocence. You are aware of your behavior and are striving toward divine innocence. Like the rest of us, you do not always succeed but you recognize when you are being the wolf.

The Wolf in Disguise: A score between 11-21 likely indicates that you are in denial about your wolfish tendencies and are likely acting as the wolf in ways that you are unaware of. You are the wolf in disguise, as the wolf who dressed as grandma in Little Red Riding Hood. The "never" response is most significant—if you consistently claim to never engage in wolfish behavior, it may indicate denial or an inability to recognize your own actions.

If you scored above 44 or under 22 on this quiz, take some time to self-reflect and seek your holy innocence through prayer and study. In this way, you can find your way back to your divine innocence and live joyfully and peacefully as your true builder type. If you feel certain that you are a stick builder, implement the techniques we have shown you here to return to innocence.

CHAPTER 4

THE BRICK PIG

Allegory of the Brick Pig

Mama was flawed but well-intentioned. She made mistakes, often without realizing the harm they caused. Still, she tried her best to create harmony in our small house. A house is just a building, but Mama worked hard to make it a home—a place of love, order, and safety. Daddy, on the other hand, was a good man but often faded into the background. He was always around, working hard to keep food on the table and the yard in order, but he rarely spoke much. I knew Daddy loved me and the rest of us piglets deeply, but I often wished he had been more present in my life. One day, though, he didn't come home. Mama told us the wolf had gotten him, and after that, I never felt safe in our family home. I miss him to this day.

I remember sitting under a tree a few days after Daddy disappeared, my head buried in my hooves as I cried. In my grief, I felt an overwhelming presence near me—something peaceful, loving, and deeply kind. It felt like someone was grieving with me, sharing my pain. At first, I thought it might be Daddy, but it didn't feel like him. Then, for the first time, I had a startling thought: could this be God? I had heard Mama mention God once, though I hadn't understood what or who He was. Now, I knew that this loving presence was God. My heart leaped with joy, and from that moment on, I understood that God was real, that He was with me, and that I belonged to Him. This realization was a gift, one that shaped my entire life.

When it was my time to leave Mama's house, I was determined to build my home out of bricks. To me, brick symbolized strength, stability, and safety. It wasn't just about the material—it was about creating a space where I could feel secure and raise a family without fear of the wolf. Brick was solid and enduring, unlike the flexible give-and-take of sticks or the lightness of straw. I was certain that a brick house would keep me and my loved ones safe from life's storms.

My decision to build with brick was rooted in something deeper than practicality. From the moment I left Mama's house, I felt a profound sense of awe at the world around me. I knew in my soul that God had created everything I saw, and this awareness gave me a strong foundation of faith. Unlike my brothers, who found faith in different ways—Bob through his courage and confidence, and Rob through his intellect and reasoning—my faith was deeply spiritual. I had an empathic connection to God that guided my life and shaped my priorities.

Faith became the cornerstone of my life. I prayed constantly, finding solace and strength in my conversations with God. I loved reading scripture and learning about divine principles. Living by the

Golden Rule—"Do unto others as you would have them do unto you"
—was my guiding principle. My faith extended beyond the walls of
any church or house of worship. It influenced every aspect of my life,
including how I treated others and how I built my home.

That said, I sometimes struggled when others didn't live by the
same principles. When people disregarded ideas like "love one
another," it was hard for me not to judge. But I tried to remind myself
that everyone is on their own path, and respecting differences is
essential to creating harmony. Despite the challenges, my ultimate goal
was always to bring harmony and order into my relationships and my
home.

As I strode away from Mama's house, I felt a sense of purpose and
excitement. I envisioned a beautiful, strong house where I could
protect my family and welcome friends. But my brothers didn't share
my enthusiasm for brick. Bob warned me that an earthquake could
topple my brick house, and Rob dismissed it as too rigid, comparing it
to a prison. Their comments stung, and I couldn't shake the feeling
that they were judging my plans unfairly.

Feeling unsettled, I went to Mama for advice. "Mama," I said,
clutching my blueprints, "Rob called my brick house a prison. I didn't
criticize his choice to build with straw. Why would he say that about
my house?"

Mama looked thoughtful. "Well, dear, that's Rob's perspective. He doesn't want to build with bricks any more than you want to build with straw. But there's something you can learn from what he said."

"What could I possibly learn from him? He's so different from me."

Mama patted the bed beside her, inviting me to sit. "It's true that bricks are strong and durable, and they'll protect you from the wolf. But be careful not to rely so much on that strength that you shut the world out. A brick house can be so sturdy that it becomes isolating. If you never leave your home or share your gifts with others, you'll miss out on the fullness of life."

"But if I stay inside, I'll never let the wolf in."

"That's true, but living in isolation isn't really living. Everyone has a deep need to express the fullness of their soul. If you isolate yourself, you might eventually grow restless. That restlessness can lead you to step out of your home in frustration, and if you're not careful, you might start trying to force others to build their homes like yours. That's when brick builders risk becoming the wolf."

Mama's words struck me deeply. I promised myself I would guard against becoming rigid or overbearing. Mama continued, "You have a special gift, Bobbie. You have a spiritual connection with God that your brothers don't have in the same way. That connection gives you authority in matters of faith, but it also comes with responsibility. Never use it to impose your beliefs on others or to see yourself as better than them. Stay in your innocence, and you'll be a beacon of light for others."

With Mama's guidance in mind, I threw myself into planning my home. I addressed my brothers' concerns by incorporating steel supports to withstand earthquakes and adding large windows to let in light, making my home feel open and inviting rather than confining. I found joy in every step of the process, from choosing an architect to overseeing the construction.

I loved orchestrating the project, watching as different experts brought their talents together to create something beautiful. My faith in God guided every decision, filling me with a sense of purpose and peace. Halfway through the construction, Rob visited me. I excitedly shared my plans, even though I could tell he didn't find them as fascinating as I did. Still, he listened patiently, and I thanked him for letting me share.

Rob surprised me by saying, "You seem to have a connection with God that I don't. It's like second nature to you." His words made me reflect on my faith in a new way. I realized that my connection with God had always been my anchor, guiding me through challenges and inspiring me to love others unconditionally.

When my home was finally complete, it was everything I had hoped for: beautiful, strong, and welcoming. The open floor plan encouraged connection, while the brick structure offered safety and peace. It was a reflection of my faith, my love for others, and my commitment to living in harmony. Brick by brick, I had built a home that stood strong against the Wolf while letting in the light of the world.

Through this journey, I learned that the strength of bricks lies not just in their durability but in their ability to create a space where love, faith, and harmony can thrive. My home was not just a refuge from the wolf; it was a place where I could share my gifts with others and live fully in the light of God's love.

Once my home was complete, I decided to celebrate with a grand party. I meticulously planned every detail, pouring the same energy and care into the event as I had into building my home. I made a list of friends and family to invite, including Rob and Bob. The menu featured delicious food, lively music, refreshing drinks, and even a karaoke machine to ensure the evening would be unforgettable. I approached the preparations with the precision of a professional event planner, determined to make everything perfect.

For weeks, I worked tirelessly, imagining how much joy the celebration would bring. The anticipation of sharing my hard work and beautiful home with loved ones filled me with excitement. However, when the day of the party arrived and my brother Rob walked in, his first comment sent a wave of irritation through me.

"Did you win the lottery?" he asked, looking around at the elaborate setup. "I mean, you have spared no expense on this party."

His words stung. My face twisted in frustration before I could stop it. Rob quickly noticed my reaction, clamping his mouth shut as if realizing he had overstepped. In that moment, I felt an overwhelming urge to ask him to leave. It was the wolf within me, howling to be let out, demanding I retaliate and tear him down for what felt like criticism. However, I knew better. Giving in to those feelings would only destroy the relationship I had with my brother.

Taking a deep breath, I decided to talk it out. "Yes," I said, "I feel criticized because 'winning the lottery' makes it sound like I spent too much."

Rob's expression softened as he realized his mistake. "I am sorry, Bobbie," he said earnestly. "I did not mean it that way. I just meant to say it is an incredible party. You have really outdone yourself. It is impressive."

His genuine apology dissolved my anger. In that moment, I saw that he appreciated my efforts and respected what I had accomplished. I also respected his willingness to acknowledge his misstep and clarify his intentions. Our conversation could have easily escalated into a conflict, but instead, it brought us closer together.

Through this experience, I realized how important communication is in preserving relationships. Poor communication, even when unintentional, can bring out the wolf in all of us. However, when we take the time to listen and understand each other, we can avoid unnecessary conflicts and build stronger connections. It is through such conversations that our unique personalities as stick, brick, or straw builders can come together harmoniously.

With the tension resolved, Rob and I rejoined the party. We grabbed plates of food and mingled with the other guests, enjoying the lively atmosphere. As I watched my friends and family laughing, eating, and singing karaoke, I could not help but feel proud of what I had created. The evening was a resounding success. Everyone complimented my efforts, and seeing their joy made all the hard work worthwhile.

Lara's Story as a Brick Builder

When I was a little girl, I loved to build things. My favorite toys were Legos, but not the specialized sets with intricate instructions and unique pieces. I preferred the simple, classic blocks that allowed me to create my own designs. I would follow long, complex instructions I imagined, building intricate creations from those basic rectangular blocks. The structured, purposeful act of building was what I enjoyed most. Playing outside felt boring by comparison. I loved to read, and by the time I was eight, I had started writing. Even today, my love for building continues—not only through stories but through big, complex projects that challenge me to bring order and beauty into the world.

My home life as a child was complicated. I grew up with a chaotic mother, an absent father, and loving grandparents who, despite their best efforts, could not shield me from the instability. That is not to say they did not help me—they did. They gave me a strong foundation in faith and a deep understanding of God. However, they could not always be there when I needed them most. My mother's drug use, narcissism, manipulative nature, and compulsive lying created a deeply traumatic and sad childhood for me.

Perhaps the most painful part was that I believed everything my mother said. It seemed as if her goal was to sabotage my success. In her eyes, the worst thing that could happen was anyone outshining her. It was not until my early forties that I discovered how much of what she told me was a lie. I suppose I believed her because it is hard to imagine that a mother would deliberately lie to her child.

Despite my chaotic home life, I excelled in school. I earned high honors and acceptance letters to some of the best colleges and universities in the country, including full scholarships to Purdue, Smith, Rensselaer Polytechnic Institute, and others. My mother, however, had other plans. She wanted me to move to Arizona with her and manipulated me into abandoning those opportunities to attend Arizona State University.

Looking back, it feels like a foolish decision, but at the time, I was utterly under her control. She told me I was too fragile to succeed at those universities without her. The truth, of course, was that she was the fragile one. I was the strong one. But I went to Arizona anyway.

Once there, I made the most of it. I enjoyed living in Arizona and eventually earned my master's degree at Virginia Tech. A similar situation occurred then—my mother discouraged me from accepting an offer from the University of Chicago, insisting once again that I would not succeed.

After graduating, I felt a deep desire to contribute to the world in meaningful ways. I became a teacher, though teaching was not a comfortable or fulfilling profession for me. I worked hard and became good at it, but I always knew I wanted to write. Eventually, I left teaching to pursue my passion, and over the years, I built my own publishing company. Through this company, I have written and edited numerous works and helped many authors achieve their dreams.

One thing about being a brick builder is that I am always working on a project. Whether it is designing a complex new system for work or building something meaningful in my personal life, I thrive when I am creating something intricate and purposeful. If I do not have a big project to work on, I feel restless. I have come to realize that my love for projects is rooted in who I am—it is how I bring harmony and order into the world.

My latest project is the most ambitious and meaningful one yet. I am building an off-grid campground and retreat center for creative people and travelers called Tickled Pink Flamingos. This project feels like the culmination of everything I have worked toward in my life. It is more than just a place—it is my life's work.

I envision Tickled Pink Flamingos as a sanctuary of peace and tranquility, a place where people can come to reconnect with their creativity, their inner selves, and the beauty of the natural world. It is located in the middle of nowhere, but that is part of its charm. It is a space where people can unplug, find inspiration, and rediscover their sense of wonder.

It has become clear to me that I may not change the whole world with my little retreat center, but maybe that is not the mission. Perhaps the purpose is to change the worlds of the people whose lives we touch. If I can help one person find peace, joy, or a renewed sense of purpose, then I have succeeded.

Today, with a grown son of whom I am incredibly proud and work that I love, I find fulfillment in building a legacy for my son and his future family. My faith in God remains my anchor. I begin every day with devotions, seeking inspiration and guidance in the Bible. My relationship with God has carried me through every challenge, and it fuels my determination to leave the world a little better than I found it.

At times, I push myself too hard. I try to accomplish more than I realistically can with the energy and resources I have. Over the years, I have had to learn my limits. Still, I am grateful for my drive to improve, to grow, and to live with purpose. For me, living without purpose—without building or creating—feels like a kind of death.

What gives my life meaning is the bigger picture of what I am building. Whether it is through my work, my writing, or Tickled Pink Flamingos, I find joy in creating something meaningful. Even if the full impact of my work is not realized in my lifetime, I find peace in knowing that I am contributing to something greater than myself.

The Brick Builder Revealed

The brick builder embodies humanity's deep need for community and collaboration, striving to create systems that support individual and societal growth. They value harmony, cooperation, and results, feeling compelled to build or participate in structures that promote collective evolution. In divine innocence, the brick builder's work is guided by God's will or their Higher Power, ensuring their efforts are rooted in truth and purpose. This section explores the defining traits of the brick builder, focusing on their role as system builders with a passion for the big picture.

Transforming Rescue to Restoration

The brick builder is the rescuer among the builder types, a role that is both vital and challenging. People occasionally need rescuing, and the brick builder is often the first to step up. However, this role requires care, as the act of rescue can easily lead to unintended consequences.

Consider the dangers of rescuing a drowning person. Without proper skills or precautions, the rescuer risks being pulled under alongside the victim. This principle became vividly clear to me (Robert) during a rafting expedition on the Nile River in Uganda. The river's strong current, combined with level four and five rapids, made the journey treacherous.

A young Ugandan man named Eric joined my group. Having never been in water before, he was understandably nervous. I reassured him, explaining the importance of staying calm if he fell into the water. I even mentioned that a panicked person might need to be subdued to prevent harm to both themselves and their rescuer.

At one point, our raft capsized, and Eric panicked. His fear was palpable as he grabbed at me, pulling at my life vest. I struggled to break free, knowing that his panic could drown us both. After a few tense moments, the current separated us, and he eventually floated into calmer waters.

This experience illustrated a profound truth: rescuing someone in a dire situation often triggers panic. The brick builder must recognize that true rescue goes beyond the immediate act—it must transition into restoration. Restoration allows the person to regain their confidence, dignity, and agency after a vulnerable moment.

An innocent brick builder focuses on facilitating this transformation. For example, if a brick builder stops to help someone with a broken-down car, they might offer immediate aid, such as a ride or assistance with repairs. However, they will also consider how to help the person restore themselves, perhaps by connecting them to job opportunities or resources to prevent future crises. This approach ensures the rescued individual regains self-respect and independence, avoiding a toxic dynamic where the rescuer becomes dominant and the rescued dependent.

The Japanese art of kintsugi, where broken pottery is repaired with gold, serves as a beautiful metaphor for this process. Instead of hiding the damage, kintsugi highlights it, creating something even more beautiful and valuable than the original. Similarly, the brick builder's restorative efforts do not erase the past but transform it into a source of strength and beauty.

The Brick Builder's Spiritual Connection

Brick builders have a natural proclivity for spirituality and a strong relationship with God or their Higher Power. This connection is foundational to their divine innocence. Brick builders inherently know God's presence and often feel guided by an inner sense of purpose.

"Faith is not passive; it is a driving force." For the brick builder, faith is not passive; it is a driving force in their lives. They view their spiritual gifts as tools to help others restore their relationship with God. Whether through formal roles such as deacons or missionaries or informal acts of kindness, brick builders are deeply committed to their spiritual mission.

Interestingly, this strong connection to spirituality can manifest in two extremes. In their innocence, brick builders live out their faith with humility and grace, drawing others toward God through their actions. In ignorance, however, they may reject spirituality entirely, often becoming outspoken critics of religion. This rejection signifies a departure from their divine innocence, as the divine presence is central to their identity.

A Powerful Personality

Among the builder types, the brick builder's personality is the most overtly powerful. They possess a natural ability to organize, lead, and bring people together. Their strength lies in their ability to focus on the big picture, working steadily toward their goals regardless of obstacles.

In innocence, the brick builder wields this power responsibly, using it to build systems and communities that uplift others. They are unshaken by challenges and remain steadfast in their purpose. Their presence commands respect, not because they seek it, but because their actions inspire trust and admiration.

However, this power can be a double-edged sword. When brick builders fall into ignorance, their strength can become oppressive.

"Brick builders use their influence to create environments where individuals can thrive, fostering trust and harmony."

They may attempt to control others, isolating themselves and those around them in the process. This deviation from innocence leads to greed, rigidity, and eventual downfall.

Innocent brick builders, by contrast,

embrace humility and recognize that their power is not their own but a gift from God. They use their influence to create environments where individuals can thrive, fostering trust and harmony.

Cultivating Freedom through Community

The brick builder's ultimate goal is to create structures that enable personal freedom and community harmony. They understand that true freedom comes from balancing individual liberty with collective well-being.

This perspective is distinct from the idea that "it takes a village to raise a child," which implies a communal control over individuals. The brick builder rejects this notion, recognizing the dangers of collectivism that stifles individuality. Instead, they seek to build systems that support and empower individuals without compromising their autonomy.

To achieve this, brick builders must guard against focusing solely on tasks or outcomes. Their efforts must remain people-centered, rooted in humility and love. By doing so, they create communities that reflect the beauty of divine innocence—places where people can grow, connect, and thrive.

The Beauty of the Brick

Innocent brick builders use their power to build beautiful spaces that allow others to freely express themselves. Their strength lies in their ability to rescue and restore without infringing on the freedom of those they help.

This requires a delicate balance. Brick builders must offer guidance and support without imposing their will or judgment on others. They rescue not by force, but through presence, encouragement, and gentle reminders of truth.

Above all, brick builders must resist the urge to judge or control others. Instead, they focus on building people up, creating spaces where everyone can flourish. By staying grounded in their divine innocence, brick builders fulfill their role as community builders, rescuers, and restorers, leaving the world better than they found it.

The Innocent Brick Builder: Faith, Vision, and Societal Evolution

An innocent brick builder has the unique ability to guide and inspire others without making them feel pressured, intimidated, or coerced into following their vision. This gentle yet firm influence stems from their faith-centered approach to life and work. For the brick builder, success is meaningless unless it aligns with a higher purpose, grounded in faithfulness and service to others. Faith, as a universal gift, is given to all in varying measures. Yet brick builders are particularly blessed with an innate, empathic connection to God that permeates their actions and decisions.

The Mastermind of Societal Evolution

Brick builders excel at creating systems and structures that bring peace, understanding, and order to the world around them. Their projects honor and uplift others, reflecting the divine nature of their work. Like architects, they are visionaries who transform intuition into actionable plans. Inspired by their connection to God, they act in faith, building something meaningful that fulfills their purpose and helps others.

Where stick builders focus on directly helping people, brick builders channel their efforts into constructing systems, environments, or institutions that empower and sustain others. They are the masterminds of societal evolution, building frameworks that promote harmony and collective growth.

Fred Rogers, the creator of Mr. Rogers' Neighborhood, exemplifies the innocent brick builder. Through his iconic television program, Rogers dedicated his life to helping children navigate a challenging world. His work reflected Christ's teaching to "love your neighbor as yourself," embodying the central tenets of his faith. Though his show was secular, Rogers' mission was deeply spiritual, rooted in his devotion to God and his belief in the transformative power of love.

Rogers once said, "The world is not always a kind place. That is something all children learn for themselves, whether we want them to or not, but it is something they really need our help to understand." This statement reflects the essence of the brick builder's purpose: to create systems that protect and guide others in a world fraught with challenges. Rogers built his program as a sanctuary of kindness, compassion, and education, equipping children with the tools to face the wolf lurking in the world. His work was an act of divine service, building harmony through children's education and love.

The Devotee of the Divine

Innocent brick builders view everything through the lens of the divine. They see the world as a manifestation of divine order and view their purpose as contributing to that order. For them, life's calling is inseparable from their role in God's kingdom.

While stick builders focus on embodying God's kingdom in action, brick builders strive to enhance it through their contributions. Their projects, goals, and efforts are always aligned with this higher vision.

Fred Rogers' life illustrates this devotion. Though he initially pursued a music composition degree, Rogers considered a career in Christian ministry. His discovery of television inspired him to use the medium as a way to reach children, helping them navigate a complex and often unkind world. Despite entering a secular career, Rogers sought ordination as a Presbyterian minister, demonstrating the brick builder's tendency to see no distinction between the sacred and the secular. For innocent brick builders, every aspect of life is part of God's order, and their work is an extension of their faith.

Building a Better World

Brick builders see themselves as stewards of God's kingdom, tasked with creating spaces where others can thrive. They understand that their work is not just about achieving personal success but about serving a higher purpose. Whether building physical structures, systems, or institutions, they seek to leave a legacy that uplifts others and reflects divine harmony.

By remaining grounded in humility and faith, innocent brick builders can harness their natural strengths to create lasting change. They inspire through their vision, lead with compassion, and build systems that honor both God and humanity. In doing so, they fulfill their calling to bring order, peace, and beauty to the world around them.

Roles of the Ignorant Brick Builder: Dominance and Rescuing

Brick builders are endowed with a tremendous gift: the ability to inspire and guide others with their empathic faith and natural leadership. However, they must be careful in how they approach others, as their powerful personalities can sometimes come across as domineering. God does not force belief on anyone; He grants people the agency to choose. Brick builders, in their divine innocence, must emulate this balance, allowing others the freedom to govern their own faith and decisions. Too much of a good thing—overzealousness or an overwhelming presence—can alienate those who lack the same gift of empathic faith.

The Dominator

The brick builder in ignorance often falls into the role of dominator, aggressively imposing their vision or beliefs on others. Though their intentions may stem from their inherent drive to create harmony, their approach can inadvertently push people away. This overbearing nature often manifests as a "my way or the highway" mentality.

Brick builders, particularly in their early stages of development, may struggle to recognize that others do not share their innate sense of harmony or their deep connection to faith. They may view dissent as a threat to their vision and respond with resentment or bitterness toward those who challenge or reject their ideas. This behavior can result in fractured relationships and a sense of isolation, as others feel coerced or undervalued in their presence.

Even in childhood, a brick personality can exhibit dominance. A child who constantly directs others or insists on their way may be expressing an early form of the brick personality. Parents who are not brick builders themselves may find this challenging. However, attempting to change the child's personality type violates their innocence and can create lasting conflict. Instead, parents must guide their child toward constructive expressions of their personality, fostering an understanding of their natural strengths while encouraging humility and empathy.

Devaluing Others

An insidious trait of the ignorant brick builder is their tendency to devalue those who disagree with them. They may unconsciously place others beneath them in a personal hierarchy, seeing dissenters as obstacles to harmony rather than individuals with valid perspectives. This devaluation often stems from a rigid view of right and wrong, where anyone outside their narrow framework is dismissed as misguided or even dangerous.

In extreme cases, the ignorant brick builder may perceive those who challenge them as enemies—traitors or anarchists who must be controlled or removed. This mindset can extend beyond individuals to institutions, governments, or societies. Organizations led by ignorant brick builders may employ propaganda or manipulation to maintain control, silencing dissent and enforcing conformity.

The Rescuer

The brick builder's natural inclination to rescue others mirrors God's role as a rescuer of souls. When approached in innocence, this instinct is a beautiful expression of their divine nature, offering help to those in need without expectation of repayment. However, when twisted by ignorance, the brick builder's rescuing tendencies can become self-serving, driven by a need for power or validation.

An ignorant brick builder may selectively choose whom to rescue, favoring those who align with their values and rejecting others. This favoritism creates a hierarchical approach to helping others, where those who fall out of favor are left behind.

Worse, the brick builder in ignorance may develop a compulsion to rescue others, seeing themselves as indispensable saviors. This dynamic often leads to unhealthy relationships, where the brick builder keeps others dependent on them rather than empowering them to stand on their own. Governments and institutions can also exhibit this behavior, creating policies that perpetuate dependency in the populace to maintain control and authority.

Personal Stories of Ignorance

One example of an ignorant brick builder's compulsion to rescue can be seen in people who fall victim to scams. In their desire to help, they may give away their life savings to someone claiming to be in need, only to realize too late that they have been exploited. This scenario highlights the dangers of unchecked rescuing behavior, where the brick builder's good intentions blind them to reality.

My father-in-law, a brick personality, lived much of his life in ignorance. Despite amassing significant wealth, he lost nearly all of it to a scam artist posing as a family friend. Even after being warned by family and friends, he refused to believe he had been deceived. His insistence on rescuing this individual stemmed from his belief in his own ethical superiority, but it ultimately led to his downfall.

This example underscores the danger of rescuing without discernment. Brick builders must balance their faith in others with critical evaluation of the facts. When they fail to do so, they risk becoming victims of their own compulsion to rescue, losing their innocence and falling into ignorance.

Ignorance in Faith

The brick builder's connection to faith is both their greatest strength and their greatest vulnerability. Those who embrace their spiritual gift often become beacons of light, using their faith to guide and restore others. However, those who reject God or misuse their faith risk falling into extremes. They may become religious zealots, imposing their beliefs on others, or they may deny God entirely, replacing divine guidance with their own flawed sense of morality.

This rejection of God can lead to deep inner turmoil. Brick builders who have experienced a spiritual awakening but turn away from it often become more irritable and combative, as they are disconnected from their core innocence. My mother, for instance, had a profound spiritual experience that frightened her so much that she rejected God entirely. This decision left her stuck in her wolf nature, unable to find peace or harmony.

Avoiding the Wolf

To remain in their innocence, brick builders must approach rescuing and leadership with humility and discernment. They should strive to empower others, offering help without creating dependency. By balancing their faith with critical evaluation and respecting the agency of others, brick builders can avoid the pitfalls of ignorance and fulfill their divine purpose.

The story of the three little pigs offers a powerful allegory for this dynamic. In many versions, the stick and straw pigs are saved by the brick pig, who shelters them in his sturdy house. While this highlights the brick builder's natural rescuing tendency, it also serves as a cautionary tale. The brick builder must be careful not to become the wolf, huffing and puffing at others' doors, imposing their will rather than offering genuine help.

Innocent brick builders rescue without expectation, guide without coercion, and create harmony through humility and love. By staying true to their divine nature, they build structures—both literal and metaphorical—that uplift and restore, creating a better world for all.

Rising Above Ignorance: The Journey to Innocence

The journey from ignorance to innocence for the brick builder begins with humility. Acknowledging their fallibility and their inability to control every external circumstance is essential. Humility allows the brick builder to see that harmony does not require uniformity or complete agreement. Instead, they must recognize that differences of opinion and perspective can contribute to a greater balance rather than threaten it.

Ignorant brick builders share the same deep faith as their innocent counterparts, but in ignorance, that faith is misplaced. Rather than placing their trust in God or a Higher Power, they place it in themselves. They believe their thoughts, feelings, and beliefs are infallible. Whether the topic is religion, career, investments, or societal issues like climate change, they see their perspective as the ultimate truth. This self-reliance becomes a barrier to innocence, as it shuts out the voices of others and disregards the freedom of others to think and live differently.

The innocent brick builder, by contrast, acknowledges the limits of their understanding and welcomes input from trusted advisors and the facts of the world around them. They accept that their faith must be informed by humility and respect for others.

Recognizing Domination

For a brick builder trapped in ignorance, it is critical to recognize when their behavior has crossed into domination. Dominance stems from the belief that they must control people and circumstances to create harmony. This belief denies the authority of God over the unknown and the uncontrollable. The ignorant brick builder assumes this authority, leading to frustration, relational discord, and, ultimately, failure.

The phrase "stay in your lane" is especially meaningful for the brick builder. It reminds them that harmony is not achieved by controlling others but by working within their own boundaries and respecting the agency of those around them.

The Trap of Rescuing

The brick builder's desire to rescue others is rooted in their empathy and motivation to create harmony. In innocence, this results in service and generosity. However, in ignorance, rescuing becomes an act of control, as the brick builder attempts to fix others' problems and create harmony on their terms.

This rescuing behavior often leads to exploitation. Many people who seek rescue are driven by unconscious motives, such as a desire for attention or control. These individuals remain in a state of neediness to maintain the dynamic that places them at the center of the brick builder's attention.

An ignorant brick builder may feel validated by rescuing others, mistaking their dependence for appreciation. However, this dynamic can quickly spiral into a situation where the brick builder sacrifices their time, energy, and resources without achieving meaningful results.

An Example of Rescuing Ignorance

When I (Robert) was younger, a woman I knew invited me over for dinner. A friend warned me against it, saying, "She is always sick." I heeded the advice and avoided further involvement. Years later, I observed that this woman had become wheelchair-bound, convinced she was a victim of circumstances. Her behavior was clearly driven by hypochondria, perhaps rooted in early trauma. Anyone who became involved with her would inevitably be drawn into a caretaker role.

An ignorant brick builder, compelled by their rescuing tendencies, might see her as someone to help, only to become trapped in a dynamic of dependence and exploitation.

The Path to Innocence

To move out of ignorance, the brick builder must first examine the motivations behind their desire to rescue. While the impulse to help comes from a place of innocence, it becomes ignorance when it leads to controlling another person's environment or decisions.

The brick builder's empathy is a unique gift. They are naturally attuned to the needs of others in ways that stick and straw builders are not. However, they must learn to serve without overstepping boundaries. When the brick builder takes on responsibilities that are not theirs, they risk creating bondage—for both themselves and the person they are trying to help.

To avoid this, the brick builder must objectively evaluate the facts of a situation. Are they truly helping someone, or are they enabling dependence? They must set clear boundaries and let go of the need to be right or in control. This requires humility and a willingness to acknowledge past mistakes.

Facing the Consequences

Ignorant brick builders often ignore facts and logic, clinging to their rescuing behavior despite clear evidence that it is harmful. To break free, they must turn inward and confront their own behavior. This includes being willing to lose relationships with those who have taken advantage of their rescuing tendencies.

Rescuing others can become an integral part of the ignorant brick builder's way of life. Their identity may be tied to their role as a rescuer, making it difficult to let go. However, by examining the results of their behavior and acknowledging the harm it has caused, they can begin to dismantle the structures of ignorance they have built.

Building a New Way of Life

On the other side of this struggle lies freedom. By deconstructing their ignorance, the brick builder can construct a new way of life centered on service rather than rescuing. This new approach respects boundaries, avoids taking responsibility for others' happiness, and focuses on empowering others rather than fixing their problems.

Brick builders in innocence understand that harmony cannot be imposed. They know that they cannot rescue everyone or create perfect harmony in every situation. Instead, they serve with humility, faith, and respect for others' autonomy.

By embracing their divine nature and letting go of their need for control, the brick builder can return to innocence. They can build a life of true harmony, one that uplifts and empowers everyone it touches.

The Brick Builders' Connection to the Father and His Commands

Among the three Persons of God, the Father plays a foundational role, ensuring the success of the Holy Spirit and Jesus the Son. In much the same way, the brick builder provides the structure that allows the stick and straw builders to thrive.

God the Father is the architect of all creation. He laid the foundations of the world and continues to orchestrate His perfect plan. Likewise, brick builders establish the groundwork for others to flourish. They are the planners, the organizers, the ones who bring harmony and order to their communities. Their task is not just to shape their own lives but to create a structure in which society itself can function peacefully and in divine innocence. This responsibility is immense, but it is not a burden to them—it is the very thing that gives them purpose. Brick builders do not merely accept their role; they thrive in it, finding deep fulfillment in constructing something lasting and meaningful.

To the other builder types, the brick builder seems almost omniscient, as if they can see the hidden mechanics of the world with uncanny precision—like a forensic accountant auditing the books. Their spiritual connection to the Father allows them to receive insights with striking clarity, often arriving as sudden realizations, patterns they intuitively understand, or even messages in dreams. When they are attuned to their divine innocence, they recognize these revelations for what they are: direct guidance from God the Father. As Yahweh Himself declared, "I am who I am." There was no elaboration, no need for further justification. The brick builder embodies this same certainty, standing firm in their convictions and taking on the responsibility of connecting others, always with the goal of benefiting the whole. This deep sense of duty fuels them into action.

However, such power must be carefully balanced. The same force that allows brick builders to create order and progress can also lead to destruction if they lose sight of their connection to the Father. A brick builder who strays from divine innocence can become rigid, controlling, and even ruthless, enforcing structure for the sake of dominance rather than unity. It is crucial that they remain anchored in their higher purpose, ensuring their strength serves others rather than consuming them.

Though the work itself is fulfilling, the truest reward for a brick builder is recognition. Just as God the Father seeks praise and glory, so too does the brick. However, the key to their divine innocence is in directing this recognition not toward themselves but toward God's work through them and the people they serve. When they remain grounded in this truth, the brick builder fulfills their divine purpose, creating lasting harmony and bringing others into alignment with the Father's grand design.

The Clear Thundering Voice of the Brick

The brick builders' voice mirrors that of Yahweh—authoritative, powerful, and direct. When the Father speaks, His intentions are clear, His words are unmistakable, and His authority is undeniable.

One of the most vivid examples of this is Yahweh's encounter with Moses at the burning bush. The Father immediately made His identity known, saying, "I am the God of your father—the God of Abraham, the God of Isaac, and the God of Jacob" (Exodus 3:6). He left no room for ambiguity, and Moses, recognizing the magnitude of the moment, fell on his face in worship and fear. This clarity and directness are hallmarks of the Father's communication style, and they are reflected in the brick builder's voice. Unlike Jesus, who often spoke in parables to encourage self-discovery, or the Holy Spirit, whose comforting whispers draw people in, Yahweh's voice commands attention with its sheer power and certainty. The brick builder's voice carries the same weight—it is confident, commanding, and impossible to ignore.

The Bible often describes Yahweh's voice as thunderous, resonating through creation with undeniable force. In Psalm 29, the psalmist vividly portrays the voice of the Lord as a force that "breaks the cedars," "strikes with flashes of lightning," "shakes the wilderness," and "twists the oaks and strips the forests bare" (Psalm 29:5-9). It is a voice of creation, power, and transformation, capable of both destruction and renewal. Similarly, the brick builder's voice is unwavering and deliberate, driven by a desire to build a better world. They speak with precision and clarity, ensuring their words leave no room for misunderstanding.

However, this strength can sometimes be misinterpreted. Other types may perceive the brick builder's confidence and conviction as overbearing or rigid. This is rarely the brick's intention. A brick builder living in divine innocence seeks not to dominate but to express truth as they understand it. Their strong, clear voice is meant to inspire and guide, not to impose. In fact, the innocent brick builder is open to hearing and incorporating others' perspectives. They are willing to be corrected or redirected because their ultimate commitment is to the truth—whatever that truth may be.

Despite this openness, others may not immediately recognize the brick builder's willingness to listen and adapt. For this reason, it can be helpful for brick builders to explicitly state their openness to new ideas or different perspectives. A simple acknowledgment of their flexibility can encourage others to engage more freely with them, fostering collaboration and mutual understanding. By balancing their strength with humility and openness, brick builders can effectively use their powerful voice to unite, guide, and build a better world.

QUIZ

ARE YOU A BRICK BUILDER?

In this section, you will have the opportunity to take a quiz to determine if you are a brick builder. This quiz is designed to separate the brick builder from other types by honing in on the core traits of the brick. Remember the caveat that we shared in the stick builder chapter: it is possible to score as a brick builder when one is actually another type if one is living inauthentically (outside of one's divine innocence).

Reflect on each of the questions below, and answer each using the following scale:

1 Never

2 Rarely

3 Sometimes

4 Often

5 Always

1. Do you organize your environment to ensure work is done efficiently and harmoniously?

   1 - 2 - 3 - 4 - 5

2. Do you consistently act on your faith in God or a Higher Power?

   1 - 2 - 3 - 4 - 5

3. If you had to relate to God the Father, Son, or Holy Spirit, would you choose God the Father?

1 - 2 - 3 - 4 - 5

4. Do you require harmony in your relationships to feel at peace?

1 - 2 - 3 - 4 - 5

5. Do you struggle to resist overpowering others in certain situations?

1 - 2 - 3 - 4 - 5

6. Do you see yourself as powerful and capable?

1 - 2 - 3 - 4 - 5

7. Do you express yourself in a way that others might describe as emphatic or strong-willed?

1 - 2 - 3 - 4 - 5

8. Is it important to you that your work has value and meaning?

1 - 2 - 3 - 4 - 5

9. Do you prioritize the appearance and organization of your home more than your own personal appearance?

1 - 2 - 3 - 4 - 5

10. Do you derive confidence and courage from your faith?

1 - 2 - 3 - 4 - 5

11. Do you view money primarily as a tool to build something bigger than yourself?

1 - 2 - 3 - 4 - 5

12. Do you often assume that others have the same knowledge or understanding as you?

    1 - 2 - 3 - 4 - 5

13. When someone attacks you repeatedly and without remorse, do you tend to cut them out of your life?

    1 - 2 - 3 - 4 - 5

14. When you meet someone, do you observe them for the purpose of judging their character (understanding that judging means evaluating in this context)?

    1 - 2 - 3 - 4 - 5

15. Do you respond best to considerate, dependable people?

    1 - 2 - 3 - 4 - 5

16. Do you find small problems irritating or even insurmountable?

    1 - 2 - 3 - 4 - 5

17. Do riddles irritate you?

    1 - 2 - 3 - 4 - 5

18. Do you enjoy setting up the foundation of an organization.

    1 - 2 - 3 - 4 - 5

How to Score Your Quiz:

If your score is between 72-90 you are most likely a brick builder living in your divine innocence. If your score was less than 72, you are most likely a different builder type.

Are You a Brick Builder Acting as the Wolf?

If your score indicates that you are a brick builder, take this quiz to determine the extent to which you are either living in innocence as the pig or ignorance as the wolf. If you are certain that you are a different type, skip this quiz and go to the next chapter.

Reflect on each of the questions below, and answer each using the following scale:

    1 Never

    2 Rarely

    3 Sometimes

    4 Often

    5 Always

1. Do you feel the need to take control because you believe others are not competent enough?

    1 - 2 - 3 - 4 - 5

2. Have you overcome chaotic periods in your life through hard work and determination?

    1 - 2 - 3 - 4 - 5

3. Do you find that life becomes chaotic when others are in control?

    1 - 2 - 3 - 4 - 5

4. Do you regularly act on faith in yourself rather than relying on others?

    1 - 2 - 3 - 4 - 5

5. If you are honest with yourself, are there chaotic or out-of-control aspects of your life that you are ignoring?

    1 - 2 - 3 - 4 - 5

6. Have you been misled into helping someone who was lying to you?

    1 - 2 - 3 - 4 - 5

7. When faced with conflict, do you respond by trying to gain greater influence over the other person?

    1 - 2 - 3 - 4 - 5

8. Have you been described as someone who adopts a "my way or the highway" attitude?

    1 - 2 - 3 - 4 - 5

9. Have people told you that you have a tendency to rescue others?

    1 - 2 - 3 - 4 - 5

10. Have you ever been an enabler for someone else's unhealthy behavior?

    1 - 2 - 3 - 4 - 5

11. Do you take on the role of rescuing people whom others tend to overlook?

    1 - 2 - 3 - 4 - 5

12. Do you enjoy being rescued yourself?

   1 - 2 - 3 - 4 - 5

13. Do you believe there are circumstances where prioritizing money is the right choice?

   1 - 2 - 3 - 4 - 5

14. Do you believe that your perspective or decisions are often better than those of others?

   1 - 2 - 3 - 4 - 5

15. When you are against someone, do you bait them to provoke outrage?

   1 - 2 - 3 - 4 - 5

How to Score the Quiz:

The Wolf: A score between 60-75 indicates more wolf-like tendencies and ignorance of your actions. You are most certainly living as the wolf if you scored in this range.

The Pig: A score between 30-59 indicates that you are living in divine innocence most of the time. Your lower score shows that you have greater awareness and commitment to living in innocence. You are aware of your behavior and are striving toward divine innocence. Like the rest of us, you do not always succeed but you recognize when you are being the wolf.

The Wolf in Disguise: A score between 15-29 likely indicates that you are in denial about your wolfish tendencies and are likely acting as the wolf in ways that you are unaware of. You are the wolf in disguise, as the wolf who dressed as grandma in Little Red Riding Hood. The "never" response is most significant—if you consistently claim to never engage in wolfish behavior, it may indicate denial or an inability to recognize your own actions.

If you scored above 44 or under 22 on this quiz, take some time to self-reflect and seek your holy innocence through prayer and study. In this way, you can find your way back to your divine innocence and live joyfully and peacefully as your true builder type. If you feel certain that you are a stick builder, implement the techniques we have shown you here to return to innocence.

CHAPTER 5

THE STRAW PIG

Allegory of the Straw Pig

Mom and Dad did their best for us. Although our lives were far from perfect, I have no complaints. Dad was a good man. He cared for us as long as he was alive, but a wolf took him from us when we were young. I often regret not having more time with him. Mom did her best to provide for us, giving us food, clothing, and an education. She encouraged us to explore our individual interests, and we each learned from her in different ways.

From a young age, I had a strong desire to understand things. Sometimes this desire made life harder for Mom. I was always curious, always asking questions. Since I process the world through action and understanding, maybe the best way to explain is to share a few memories.

"I will be down in a moment, Mom," I squealed.

"This is the third time you have said that!" Mom called back, exasperated.

I could tell she was waiting, probably worried about the food getting cold. Most likely, Bob and Bobbie were waiting for me, too, but I just could not pull myself away.

"Are you still reading the dictionary?" Mom asked.

If I answered, I knew she would make me come immediately, so I kept quiet.

"What letter are you reading about?" she asked.

"Q," I called back.

I heard her footsteps coming down the hall. When she appeared in the doorway, her round figure filled the frame. She crossed her arms and sighed.

I sat up, excited to share. "Did you know there are only a few words in English that have a 'Q' standing alone in their spelling? And most 'Q's are followed by a 'U,' which makes a queue sound."

Mom tilted her head. "I did not know that."

"And," I continued, "in other languages where the 'Q' stands alone, it often makes a K sound. Isn't that fascinating?"

Mom gave a small smile. "You are excited to learn everything you can, aren't you?"

"Yes!" I said. "I want to know everything so I can become the best dentist ever."

"I believe you, Rob," she said warmly.

I beamed. "And guess what else? I have been studying straw because I want to build my house out of it someday. That will make the best house, right?"

Mom frowned slightly. "Are you sure you want to build a house out of straw?"

"Yes, Mom. Did you know that straw does not grow as straw?"

"It does not?"

"No! Straw is actually the stem of a plant, mostly from grains like wheat or barley. After the plant sends nutrients to its seeds, the stem becomes a by-product. It is spent, like a tree trunk after it sends nourishment to its leaves."

"Oh my," Mom murmured.

I took a deep breath and kept going. "Straw is tough and fibrous, and while it is not good to eat, it is very strong. And when you weave straw together, it becomes even stronger. That is why our cousin's straw house got blown down by the wolf—he did not weave the straw properly or use the right kind."

Mom nodded. "You remembered the story well."

I straightened proudly. "Ever since Dad was eaten by the wolf, I have been determined to build a straw house that the wolf cannot blow down."

Mom gave me a long look. "That is a good idea, Rob. But did you make your bed today?"

I froze. Her question caught me off guard. Who cared about my bed? "No," I admitted.

"Rob, we have talked about this. You need to keep your room tidy."

"But why?" I protested. "I am just going to mess it up again tonight."

Mom sighed. "Because success in life requires patience and perseverance. Now go make your bed and come back to tell me more stories."

I ran upstairs, yanked the covers over my bed, and smoothed them hastily. Then I rushed back to Mom. "Did you know," I began breathlessly, "there are so many kinds of straw besides wheat and barley? Farmers often use it for bedding, thatching roofs, insulation, even making hats. And some straw, like hemp or raffia, is incredibly strong and versatile."

"You have been doing your research," Mom said.

I nodded eagerly. "It is the fiber and the weave that make it so strong. If our cousin had woven his straw, he might have survived. But he just piled it up, and the wolf blew it away."

Mom's expression softened. "I am glad you are learning from reliable sources. You are very intelligent, Rob."

Her praise filled me with pride. "That means a lot, Mom. I think I can learn even more from experts and by studying others' experiences. That is the smartest way to gain knowledge, right?"

"Yes," she agreed.

"And how will I know I am not being deceived?" I asked.

Mom sat beside me on the bed. "You will know through your innocence, Rob. The wolf overpowered your cousin because he acted in ignorance. He thought he had the right knowledge, but he did not verify it. This is why you must always double-check your findings and stay humble in your learning."

I nodded slowly, trying to absorb her wisdom.

"Keep your innocence sacred, Rob," she continued. "Be honest in your interactions. Learn from your mistakes, and stay true to your values. That is how you will protect yourself from the wolf."

Her words stayed with me as I grew older and prepared to build my own home. I knew I wanted a straw house because it was adaptable and easy to repair. But I also felt anxious. What if I failed? What if the wolf came?

One night, as I sat poring over books on house building, Mom knocked on my door. "Rob?" she said gently.

I glanced up.

"What's wrong, honey?"

"I don't know," I muttered.

Mom came in and sat beside me. "Are you worried about building your home?"

I nodded.

"You are scared because you do not know how things will turn out," she said. "But you have done new things before, and you can do this, too. You just need to trust yourself."

"But what if I make a mistake?"

"Straw is forgiving," she reminded me. "If you make a mistake, you can fix it. The key is to take your time and not cut corners."

Her reassurance gave me the courage I needed. I began building my house the next week. Though the process was slow, I worked carefully, weaving the straw into sturdy walls. When it was finished, I moved in quietly, without the fanfare my siblings loved.

To this day, my straw house stands strong. It is easy to repair and flexible enough to suit my needs. I am proud of what I built, and I know that if the wolf ever comes, he will not blow my house down.

The Dentist's Story as a Straw Builder

Of all medical professions, straw builders, who value efficiency, are most likely to pursue careers such as dentistry or becoming a physician's assistant. Straw builders excel in medical fields, regardless of specialty, due to their attention to detail and relentless pursuit of knowledge. A straw builder dentist, for example, would be highly knowledgeable and adept at fixing teeth correctly, quickly, and efficiently while using the highest-quality materials. Their quickness pleases most patients, who are eager to minimize the time spent with hands in their mouths. Once the problem is resolved, the straw builder dentist is ready to move on to the next tooth or patient, satisfied with their efficient work.

Dentists of other builder types might bring different challenges. A brick builder dentist may focus less on efficiency and more on encouraging additional services or treatments, often with the aim of building a long-term relationship or practice growth. A stick builder, however, might find the repetitive nature of dentistry tiresome, leading to dissatisfaction with the profession. For this reason, straw builders often make the most natural dentists. Their blend of efficiency, practicality, and attention to detail is uniquely suited to the demands of the profession.

Take my acquaintance Chen as an example. When I asked Chen which type of house he would build, he immediately chose straw. For him, the decision was clear. Much like fixing a tooth, he wanted to construct his house efficiently and move on to other areas of his life that captured his interest. Chen quickly envisioned a plan to build a home that would be strong, sturdy, and efficient, proving that straw, far from being an inferior material, could be perfectly suitable for a straw builder like himself. To Chen, building with straw mirrored his approach to dentistry: solving problems quickly and moving forward with purpose.

Chen is exceptionally smart and resourceful. Growing up, he observed the struggles of his parents—his mother, a fanatically religious brick builder, and his father, who held similarly rigid values.

Chen's father was so frugal that he would salvage food from dumpsters to feed the family. If the food was unsuitable for humans, he would compost it in the garden. These experiences had a profound impact on Chen, shaping his determination to live a better life. He made a firm decision early on that once he had control over his circumstances, he would pursue a path that provided stability, independence, and efficiency.

Chen's childhood observations, coupled with his own experiences, became the foundation for his life plan. As a straw builder, he naturally gravitated toward strategies that allowed him to achieve his goals quickly and effectively. He analyzed the failures of others—including his parents—and used those lessons to inform his decisions. At the same time, Chen understood that his learning would not be complete without personal experience. He accepted that making mistakes was an essential part of growth. As long as the wolf did not consume him, Chen knew he could view failures as valuable opportunities to learn and improve.

What set Chen's divine innocence apart was his pragmatic approach to life. When he graduated from college, he enrolled in a three-year dental program instead of the traditional four-year route. The shorter program allowed him to start practicing sooner, a decision that perfectly aligned with his efficiency-driven personality. Chen worked hard during those three years, focusing on mastering the skills and knowledge necessary to become a successful dentist.

Chen's path reflects the core traits of a straw builder. He understood the importance of balancing observation with action, planning with execution, and efficiency with thoroughness. His story illustrates how the straw builder's desire for practicality and speed, when coupled with divine innocence, can lead to both professional success and personal fulfillment.

The Straw Builder Revealed

If you are a straw builder, or if you have one in your life, this chapter is for you. Ironically, many straw builders may have stopped reading this book by now. Their natural impatience, combined with their preference for data over theory, often leads them to move on quickly unless they are highly motivated to stay engaged. However, if you are still reading, thank you. This section is designed to help straw builders and those who love them better understand how they express their divine innocence and how their unique traits benefit themselves and others.

Pursuers of Truth

Straw builders are passionate pursuers of truth. To them, life is a series of puzzles, games, or even a matrix waiting to be unraveled. They thrive on gathering information, researching their areas of interest, and solving problems with precision and efficiency. Their identity is deeply tied to their knowledge, which they see as an essential part of who they are. They take pride in becoming authorities in their chosen fields, and they approach the world with a sense of enlightenment, recognizing their capacity for intellectual depth.

In their divine innocence, straw builders understand that their authority is always evolving. While it may be difficult to change their minds, it is never impossible with the right combination of credible evidence and compelling arguments. However, when they fall into ignorance, they see their knowledge as absolute, and questioning their ideas becomes a direct threat to their identity. To deny a straw builder's wisdom is to invite the wolf within them to emerge.

This dynamic extends to interactions with children who have straw builder personalities. Parents, for instance, are better off guiding a straw child through questions rather than issuing direct commands. Imagine a parent catching their child eating a crayon. Instead of saying, "Do not eat that," they might ask, "Is that food?" If the child insists it is food, the parent can gently steer them toward recognizing that the crayon is only food in their imagination. This approach encourages the child to arrive at the correct conclusion themselves, preserving their autonomy and fostering their innocence. This technique is particularly effective with straw builders, even from a young age, though it may not work as well with stick or brick personalities.

The straw builder's approach to truth and learning mirrors the Socratic Method, which uses questions and logical progression to lead

"The Socratic Method relies on the authority of the teacher to guide students toward mastery, which is a concept straw builders instinctively resonate with."

students to their own discoveries. Socrates himself may well have been a straw builder, given his reliance on dialogue and reason to uncover deeper truths. The Socratic Method relies on the authority of the teacher to guide students toward mastery, which is a concept straw builders instinctively resonate with. They respect the process of rational inquiry and appreciate being led to their own conclusions, as long as they trust the authority guiding them.

Communication with Straw Builders

If you have a straw builder in your life, it is important to understand how they communicate and how they interpret interactions. Straw builders value their intellectual contributions and prefer to express their ideas in a gentle, measured way. However, they can easily feel disregarded or disrespected if others bulldoze over their thoughts or interrupt them. This can lead to disengagement, even when they are operating in innocence.

To encourage open dialogue with a straw builder, validate their ideas rather than bluntly challenging them. Simple affirmations, such as "hmm" or "interesting," can go a long way in keeping the conversation productive and harmonious. While these responses may feel insincere, they help prevent the wolf from surfacing in the discussion. Straw builders prefer to tell rather than be told, and they appreciate when their knowledge is acknowledged and respected. Dismissing or second-guessing their ideas is a surefire way to push them into ignorance.

Training Over Teaching

Straw builders are naturally drawn to training rather than traditional teaching. While both methods are important, training aligns more closely with the straw builder's personality. Teaching is often abstract, theoretical, and hierarchical, with a clear distinction between teacher and student. In contrast, training is hands-on and collaborative, with the understanding that the student will eventually become the teacher's equal.

This distinction is critical for straw builders, who tend to set impossibly high expectations for their teachers. They demand exceptional depth of knowledge and mastery from those they learn from, and once they feel they have surpassed a teacher's expertise, they lose respect for them. This loss of respect is nearly impossible to regain. By contrast, trainers, who position themselves as mentors or collaborators rather than ultimate authorities, are more likely to maintain a straw builder's trust and engagement.

Straw builders express their pursuit of knowledge in three primary ways:

1. Pursuing Higher Education: Many straw builders thrive in academic settings, where they value the structure and credentials of formal education. However, their teachers must continually prove their expertise to earn the straw builder's respect.

2. Mastering a Trade: Others prefer hands-on learning through apprenticeships or certification programs, where they gain practical skills and knowledge directly from experienced mentors.

3. Self-Teaching: Some straw builders take an independent approach, using the internet and other resources to educate themselves. These autodidacts value efficiency and flexibility but may experience loneliness due to the lack of community found in more traditional learning environments.

Status by Association vs. Reputation by Action

Innocent straw builders build their reputations through their actions rather than seeking status by association. They value their accomplishments over external validation and do not feel the need to name-drop or rely on affiliations with prestigious institutions to bolster their identity. They assess others based on their depth of knowledge and contributions, not on their social or professional status.

In ignorance, however, straw builders may fall into the trap of valuing status as a substitute for genuine accomplishment. They might display certificates, degrees, or other symbols of success as a way to broadcast their worth. This reliance on external validation often stems from insecurity and can lead to an endless pursuit of recognition that never truly satisfies.

Autodidacts, who rely on self-teaching rather than formal education, are less likely to seek status by association. However, they may develop a sense of superiority based on their ability to independently discern truth. This can create its own challenges, as they may struggle to connect with others who do not share their methods or values.

The Innocent Straw Builder

At their core, innocent straw builders are calm, collected, and confident in their abilities. They view truth as an ever-evolving concept and remain open to refining their ideas when presented with credible evidence. This humility allows them to build meaningful connections with others and avoid the pitfalls of arrogance or division.

In contrast, ignorant straw builders become rigid and dismissive, clinging to their knowledge as absolute and rejecting any challenge as a personal attack. They may devalue others' opinions and prioritize their own authority above all else. To maintain their innocence, straw builders must focus on collaboration, humility, and a willingness to learn from others.

By embracing their divine innocence, straw builders can use their knowledge and curiosity to contribute meaningfully to their communities. They are natural problem-solvers, innovators, and researchers, capable of seeing connections and solutions that others might miss. When they operate in innocence, their pursuit of truth becomes a gift not only to themselves but to everyone around them.

Roles of the Innocent Straw Builder

Knowledge Seeker and Wise Teacher

Among the three builder types, straw builders are the most likely to be impressed by status and titles. However, this inclination is not inherently outside of divine innocence. Status and titles are not inherently negative or indicative of ignorance; they serve as societal tools for categorization, organization, and managing collective action. Innocent straw builders recognize this and avoid using status or titles as a form of posturing. Instead, they see these markers as symbols of the knowledge and skills they represent. When achievements are rooted in diligence, merit, hard work, intelligence, and a respectful acknowledgment of innocence, the status they confer is genuinely earned and deserved. In such cases, financial rewards are innocently accepted as the natural outcome of those accomplishments.

Straw builders' deep connection to information often makes them appear like "know-it-alls," particularly when their personalities devolve into ignorance. Even in innocence, straw builders frequently use phrases such as "I know" or "Did you know?" Their strong emphasis on authenticated authority allows them to confidently validate their insights and act decisively. This confidence is a hallmark of their gifted innocence.

Straw builders are passionate about what they know—and even about what they think they know—to the extent that they will defend their conclusions fiercely if challenged. Historically, this trait can be seen in figures like Galileo, who risked everything to defend his controversial, evidence-based beliefs. To straw builders, facts are immutable and worth protecting. This does not mean that all straw builders blindly champion science or any particular discipline. Their conclusions are shaped by their training, experiences, and the credibility of those they trust. Straw builders place immense value on reliability and integrity, aligning themselves with individuals or systems that have earned their respect and remained steadfast in their commitments.

Investigator/Detective

Straw builders are natural investigators. When embarking on a project, they instinctively gather as much information as possible, working diligently to separate fact from fiction. For them, information is the key to making sound decisions. They strive to uncover every relevant detail, analyzing data to reach accurate conclusions. This drive to know can sometimes lead to an overwhelming realization: it is impossible to gather every single fact. As a result, straw builders may fall into the trap of "analysis paralysis," becoming unable to decide because they are fixated on acquiring more data.

Despite this, investigation is a profound gift of the straw builder. In a team setting, they excel at uncovering historical context and relevant facts for projects. Unlike brick builders, who enjoy theoretical exploration, straw builders are uninterested in hypotheticals or untested theories. Instead, they are grounded in concrete data and real-world application. Ironically, while straw builders are adept at uncovering and compiling information, they are not always skilled at synthesizing it into actionable plans. Their passion lies in the process of discovery itself, while the act of implementing their findings often feels tedious or uninspiring. For straw builders, taking action can seem like a chore, leading to impatience with the follow-through.

Delegator

Of the three builder types, straw builders are the most natural delegators. They are quick to pass on responsibilities, preferring to focus on gathering information rather than executing tasks. They are also more inclined to abdicate leadership roles, making them better managers than leaders. Several traits contribute to this tendency.

First, straw builders are inherently impatient. They recognize that delegating tasks to others is often quicker and more efficient than completing the work themselves. Their preference for sharing responsibilities contrasts sharply with brick builders, who often desire control over the process and will delegate only when necessary. Brick builders thrive on managing and executing tasks to ensure the process aligns with their vision, while straw builders are content to focus on information gathering and leave the action to others.

This preference for delegation can sometimes lead to the misconception that straw builders are lazy. In reality, they are not lazy —they simply prioritize their energy toward intellectual pursuits, learning, and exploration. Their natural inclination is to seek knowledge and novel experiences rather than engage in routine or repetitive tasks. By delegating, straw builders free themselves from mundane responsibilities, allowing them to focus on discovering and analyzing new information.

Trailblazers of New Horizons

Straw builders' aversion to repetition and routine stems from their desire for novelty. They thrive on blazing trails and uncovering uncharted territories, leaving the construction and establishment of their discoveries to brick and stick builders. For example, a straw builder might explore a new idea, outline its potential, and then delegate its implementation to someone else. This preference for innovation over execution allows straw builders to continue expanding their horizons without becoming bogged down by the details of operational follow-through.

This dynamic is essential to understanding the unique role straw builders play in any team or community. They provide the critical groundwork of information, insight, and discovery that enables others to act. Their curiosity, resourcefulness, and passion for learning are the sparks that ignite larger initiatives. However, their impatience and preference for delegation mean they are most effective when paired with stick and brick builders, who can bring their visions to fruition.

Roles of the Ignorant Straw Builder

Name Dropper and Status Seeker

When straw builders fall into ignorance, they become prone to name-dropping and status-seeking. For example, an ignorant straw builder might boast, "I met Michael Jackson in person." The details—how, why, or when—are irrelevant to them. The encounter might have been as trivial as seeing him in a parking lot from a distance. To the ignorant straw builder, the name is what matters, not the context. Similarly, they might emphasize who they associate with, saying things like, "I only do business with millionaires." Designer brands are another way they seek to assert status, whether it is through wearing clothing with prominent logos or using brand names in conversation.

This behavior is not inherently ignorant. Wearing designer clothes, sharing celebrity encounters, or marketing one's business to affluent clients is not problematic on its own. It becomes an issue when the straw builder ties their sense of identity and self-worth to these associations. For them, these connections and symbols of status become evidence of their value, and they judge others by the same standard. The ignorant straw builder is more likely to dismiss people who do not prioritize status because they view status and associations as proof of what is true, important, and real.

This constant pursuit of status is not only costly but damaging to the soul. When the ignorant straw builder bases their identity on external markers like name-dropping or titles, they are left perpetually chasing validation. They cannot rest, fearing they will be exposed as unworthy of the status they claim. They mistrust their divine innocence, which could provide the security, confidence, and peace they seek. Instead, they look outward, searching for external validation to fill the void within.

This behavior can have particularly negative effects on children raised by ignorant straw builders. Parents or caregivers who demand that their children achieve specific titles or status can erode their children's innocence and push them toward a life of ignorance. Such expectations create undue pressure, leading children to feel they must deny their authentic selves to meet their parents' standards. This dynamic can cause resentment, rebellion, or worse outcomes.

An extreme example of this occurred in the Hacking family of Utah. The parents, a pediatrician and a nurse, placed immense pressure on their children to achieve high-status careers. Most of their children became doctors, lawyers, and scientists, but one son, Mark, did not conform. Desperate to please his family, he lied, claiming to have graduated from the University of Utah and been accepted to medical school. When his wife discovered the truth, Mark's fear of exposure drove him to murder her. While his actions were entirely his responsibility, they underscore the dangers of placing excessive emphasis on status and external validation.

Blind Activist

In ignorance, straw builders can become blind activists, rigidly adhering to a single line of thought based on incomplete information. Their reliance on data and facts often leads them to believe their conclusions are absolute, even when they lack the full picture. This is particularly true when they make predictions about the future. If their predictions fail, instead of reevaluating their position, they move the goalposts to fit their narrative. They cling to their conclusions because those beliefs have become intertwined with their identity. To challenge their position is to challenge their sense of self.

This rigidity can lead to destructive behaviors. Ignorant straw builders may attack anything that does not align with their worldview, often without considering other perspectives. For example, they might join movements that destroy symbols or institutions they perceive as contrary to their beliefs, even if they are not personally connected to those symbols. They act with a distorted sense of righteousness, believing it is their duty to force others to conform to their version of truth.

Ironically, their intolerance often extends to the very concept of tolerance. A blindly activist straw builder may passionately advocate for universal tolerance while simultaneously being intolerant of anyone who holds opposing views. This paradox arises from their deep attachment to their ideology, which blinds them to the broader implications of their actions.

In their quest to champion their cause, ignorant straw builders often fixate on a single enemy—whether a person, group, or institution. They become so consumed with their hatred for this target that they lose sight of the principles they initially sought to defend. They may even ally with others who contradict their beliefs simply because they share a common adversary. This misplaced focus further entrenches their ignorance and damages their relationships and credibility.

The Cost of Ignorance

The ignorant straw builder's reliance on external validation and rigid beliefs erodes their divine innocence. Instead of trusting their innate ability to discern truth and value, they become trapped in cycles of insecurity and external dependence. This insecurity manifests in behaviors like name-dropping, status-seeking, and blind activism, all of which are attempts to bolster their fragile ego.

In the workplace, this ignorance can lead to posturing and a need to prove oneself through titles or accomplishments. For example, an ignorant straw builder might prominently display their degrees or certifications, not as a celebration of their achievements but as a shield against perceived inadequacy. While these behaviors may temporarily boost their confidence or authority, they ultimately weaken their soul and push them further from their divine identity.

Parents who embody this ignorance can inadvertently become the "wolf" in their children's lives. By using their authority to demand compliance—statements like "Because I am your mother, that is why!"—they undermine their children's sense of self and train them to prioritize external validation over internal integrity. Such authoritarian parenting fosters a cycle of ignorance, passing down the very insecurities that drive the parents' behavior.

Breaking Free

To move out of ignorance, straw builders must learn to trust their divine innocence. This requires letting go of the need for external validation and embracing the mystery of their innate identity. Divine innocence is not something that can be mastered or fully understood—it is something to rest in. It provides peace, security, and clarity, allowing straw builders to pursue truth without fear of failure or judgment.

By reconnecting with their innocence, straw builders can break free from the traps of name-dropping, status-seeking, and blind activism. They can embrace their natural curiosity and intelligence as gifts to be shared rather than weapons to defend themselves. In doing so, they will find that their worth is not tied to what they know or who they associate with but to the divine spark within them that makes them unique.

The Straw Builder's Path to Divine Innocence

Truth—and access to it—is the cornerstone of the straw builder's perspective. A straw builder operating in divine innocence understands that no human being has access to all truth. They accept and even embrace the limitations of their knowledge, both in themselves and in others. The innocent straw builder's unique role is to teach and learn from all perspectives without criticism or judgment. They work to understand the viewpoints of others, allowing themselves to grow from the exchange. They do not require absolute proof of value to accept people or ideas.

By contrast, the ignorant straw builder operates from arrogance, mistaking their opinions, feelings, and knowledge for absolute truth. The wolf within emerges when they aggressively promote their perspective as the only truth and demonize others for disagreeing. In this section, we explore how the search for truth can help the ignorant straw builder shift their perspective and live in divine innocence.

The Power of Introspection

If the ignorant straw builder were to turn their analytical mindset inward, they would uncover their errors. This act of introspection is one path back to innocence. They often claim their actions are based on 'facts' from reliable information and credible authorities while criticizing others for failing to do the same. If they were to consider— even as a thought experiment—that others' information and authorities could be valid, they would gain a new understanding of how others form their beliefs, even if those beliefs are flawed. This perspective fosters compassion, wisdom, and the ability to relate to others without judgment. Furthermore, it would help the straw builder recognize and correct their own mistakes, ultimately making them wiser and more knowledgeable.

However, many ignorant straw builders resist this introspection because it feels like an attack on their identity. To them, questioning their knowledge or chosen authorities is as invasive as a thief breaking into their home. They perceive these challenges as existential threats and respond with hostility, unable to let the perceived violation go. This tendency to defend their worldview at all costs is unique to the straw builder's personality type. Yet, if they could accept the inherent incompleteness of all knowledge, they would transform from blind activists into passionate seekers of truth, benefiting society with their exceptional ability to research, analyze, and share evolving understandings.

The journey from ignorance to divine innocence requires the straw builder to embrace open-mindedness. They must allow themselves to be influenced by diverse perspectives, even those they initially disagree with. This can be a daunting shift because straw builders often fear being wrong. Their deep need for truth, while a strength, can also paralyze them when faced with uncertainty. They may avoid decisions altogether, worried about making the wrong choice. To overcome this fear, the straw builder must recognize the universal human limitation: it is impossible to have all the information. This acknowledgment allows them to step outside their self-created echo chambers, where they surround themselves with agreement and absolutes. In doing so, they reconnect not only with others but also with the very pursuit of truth that energizes them.

The straw builder's impatience can compound their ignorance. Seeking quick results, they may resort to shortcuts like name-dropping, status-seeking, or clinging to authoritative figures. These shortcuts provide a false sense of confidence, but they lack the substance of true understanding. For instance, straw builders are more likely to employ illogical arguments, such as the straw man fallacy, to win debates. The straw man involves exaggerating or distorting an opponent's position to make it easier to refute. While this tactic may temporarily bolster the straw builder's confidence, it ultimately undermines their integrity and deepens their ignorance. To move toward divine innocence, the straw builder must reject these shortcuts and commit to the more challenging path of authentic learning and self-reflection.

True confidence begins with humility, which is perhaps the hardest step for any builder type. Pride—the belief that one has all the answers—is the root of all ignorance. It blinds the straw builder to their limitations and keeps them trapped in arrogance and insecurity. By embracing humility, they can accept that their knowledge is always incomplete. This acceptance is not a weakness but a shared human experience. It is through this humility that the straw builder can partner with the divine, accessing wisdom far greater than their own.

Rooted in the Holy Spirit

In divine innocence, the straw builder's connection to truth mirrors the Christian concept of the Holy Spirit: a breath, a wind, a source of divine intelligence that guides and enlightens. At Pentecost, the Holy Spirit enabled the apostles to speak to a diverse crowd, with each listener understanding in their own language. Similarly, the innocent straw builder taps into a universal source of wisdom that allows them to approach truth with openness and clarity. This connection requires trust in the divine, recognizing that they can never fully understand the infinite. By resting in this trust, the straw builder finds peace and clarity in their pursuit of truth.

The ignorant straw builder, however, often seeks validation through external markers like status and titles. They may name-drop celebrities, flaunt designer brands, or emphasize connections to prestigious institutions. While these behaviors are not inherently wrong, they become problematic when used to define self-worth. The ignorant straw builder relies on these external symbols to compensate for a lack of inner confidence, creating a cycle of insecurity. They are constantly chasing new markers of status to maintain their self-image. To break free, the straw builder must recognize that true value comes from within and is rooted in their divine nature, not external accomplishments.

Relationships often suffer when the straw builder prioritizes status. Parents, for instance, may place undue pressure on their children to achieve high-status roles, disregarding the child's individuality. This can lead to rebellion, resentment, or even complete estrangement. To return to innocence, the straw builder must learn to value people for who they are rather than what they achieve, fostering relationships built on mutual respect and understanding.

Impatience is another challenge for the ignorant straw builder, particularly in decision-making. Overwhelmed by options and the fear of making the wrong choice, they may experience analysis paralysis, endlessly researching without acting. To overcome this, the straw builder must embrace the idea that no decision is perfect. Mistakes are opportunities for growth, and taking action—even imperfect action—is essential for learning. By viewing life as a series of experiments rather than a test of perfection, they can move forward with confidence and curiosity.

Straw builders are also prone to disengaging from conversations or relationships they find inefficient or unproductive. In ignorance, they may quickly lose interest and withdraw, isolating themselves. The innocent straw builder, on the other hand, learns to listen and engage, even when the interaction does not align with their preferences. They understand that meaningful relationships require patience and effort and that these investments are essential for personal growth.

Ultimately, the journey from ignorance to divine innocence is about balance. The straw builder must balance their drive for efficiency with the patience to build meaningful connections. They must temper their pursuit of truth with humility, recognizing that they are part of a larger, infinitely intelligent universe. In doing so, they fulfill their role as stewards of wisdom, contributing to a world that values knowledge, understanding, and compassion.

Letting Go of External Validation

The straw builder's strength lies in their internal connection to truth, but they become weak when they seek validation through external markers like status or titles. For the straw builder to maintain their divine innocence, they must recognize that their worth and wisdom are inherent, rooted in their divine nature. This requires them to develop a strong relationship with their inner consciousness, taking their nebulous feelings and thoughts seriously. Balancing their drive to know observable facts with the cultivation of their inner world is essential. This balance is greatly supported by a relationship with God. In divine innocence, the straw builder accepts God for who God is, without needing to fully explain or understand the infinite.

An innocent straw builder acknowledges their finite nature and the impossibility of fully comprehending the infinite mind of God. Conversely, the ignorant straw builder denies their reliance on God for truth, leading them to the irrational belief that they either have access to all truth or that truth itself does not exist because they cannot grasp it entirely.

Embracing Alternate Perspectives

To move toward divine innocence, the straw builder must be willing to consider the validity of other points of view, even those they have not personally verified. While they do not have to adopt these perspectives, they must respect them and engage with others in a way that builds rapport, regardless of differences. This openness enables the straw builder to step away from rigid, dogmatic thinking and instead fulfill their divine role as stewards of wisdom.

Managing Impatience and Efficiency

Straw builders are often impatient and highly focused on efficiency, more so than other builder types. They aim to complete tasks as quickly and with as little effort as possible. When faced with inefficiency, they may feel paralyzed, expending significant energy to improve processes even when it would have been easier to simply complete the task inefficiently. However, this trait can lead to breakthroughs, as their focus often results in innovative systems that save time in the long run. Henry Ford's development of the assembly line serves as a prime example of this trait in action. Though it was initially difficult to implement, Ford's persistence revolutionized manufacturing, leaving a lasting impact.

When managed properly, impatience and efficiency can benefit both society and the workplace. However, if the straw builder becomes dogmatic or dismissive, these traits can lead to shortcuts that compromise the quality of their work. This is why disciplines like annual recertification for medical professionals are particularly well-suited to the straw builder. Such systems align with their respect for authority and ensure that their work maintains a high standard over time.

Impatience in Relationships

Impatience also affects the straw builder's relationships. Ignorant straw builders often lose interest in conversations that deviate from their preferred focus on efficiency or data-driven topics. They may quickly disengage from discussions that seem overly emotional or meandering, finding small talk or "chatter" particularly grating. For them, the sooner a conversation gets to the point, the better.

Innocent straw builders, on the other hand, recognize this tendency and work to overcome it. They allow others to express themselves fully, even if the conversation veers away from their interests. While they may not become naturally chatty, they develop the ability to actively listen, making others feel heard and valued. This effort to engage with different communication styles prevents relational breakdowns and strengthens connections.

Addressing Name Dropping and Status Seeking

A significant step toward divine innocence involves addressing the straw builder's inclination toward name dropping and status seeking. These behaviors often arise from an inner need for validation when the straw builder feels disconnected from their divine nature. By associating themselves with social icons, material possessions, or institutional accolades, the ignorant straw builder attempts to bolster their sense of self-worth.

To move past this, straw builders must first acknowledge what drives these habits: a search for truth and validation. In the absence of true inner confidence, they settle for external markers of acceptance provided by society. However, these symbols only offer temporary reassurance and can ultimately leave the straw builder feeling hollow and dependent on others' approval.

The innocent straw builder recognizes that true worth and validation come from within, through their connection to the divine. This realization enables them to stop idolizing or dismissing individuals based on social status, wealth, or opinions. Instead, they learn to engage with all people respectfully and genuinely, regardless of societal labels.

Interestingly, the ignorant straw builder may also use status symbols as a rhetorical tool, believing that they strengthen their arguments. In reality, these references often emotionalize discussions, undermining the logical foundation of their points. To return to innocence, the straw builder must shift their focus away from external validation and toward alignment with divine truth.

Overcoming Analysis Paralysis

Straw builders are particularly prone to analysis paralysis, the inability to make decisions due to an overwhelming amount of information. This tendency arises from their desire to make the "perfect" choice, combined with their fear of making mistakes. Whether they are selecting a college, choosing a career, or even deciding where to eat, they can get stuck in an endless cycle of research and overthinking.

To overcome this, innocent straw builders must accept that no decision is perfect and that life is inherently a process of learning and adaptation. By viewing mistakes as opportunities for growth, they can free themselves from the need for perfection and begin to trust their intuition alongside their research. This shift allows them to make decisions more confidently and in a timely manner.

Valuing Collaboration

Another key to divine innocence is learning to value collaboration and accept others' roles in decision-making. Straw builders often struggle to trust others' judgments, particularly when they perceive gaps in knowledge or logic. However, when they recognize the benefits of teamwork and diverse perspectives, they can release the burden of having to know and do everything themselves.

This acceptance is deeply tied to their relationship with a Higher Power. By acknowledging that God is guiding them and others, straw builders can let go of their need for control. This faith in a greater plan provides them with the security to navigate uncertainty and to trust that others can contribute meaningfully to shared goals.

Embracing Experimentation

To fully embrace their divine innocence, straw builders must integrate their love for research and knowledge with a willingness to experiment and take action. Life is not a static collection of facts but a dynamic process of discovery and growth. By approaching life with curiosity and humility, straw builders can see mistakes not as failures but as valuable data points that enhance their understanding.

Innocent straw builders engage with others from a place of openness and respect, valuing diverse viewpoints and fostering relationships that enrich their pursuit of truth. Their actions align with their divine purpose, allowing them to contribute meaningfully to the world while remaining grounded in their inner strength.

By balancing their drive for knowledge with faith in the divine and trust in their own innocence, straw builders transcend the limitations of ignorance and step into their full potential as stewards of wisdom and truth. In doing so, they not only transform their own lives but also inspire and uplift those around them.

The Straw Builder's Connection to the Holy Spirit and His Whispers

Straw builders possess a profound connection with the Holy Spirit, one that shapes their perception of the world and their pursuit of truth. The Spirit whispers to them a desire for knowledge, precision, and validation, embedding divine wisdom into their very being.

Because straw builders in divine innocence are so attuned to the Spirit, they can perceive the tangible world through a lens that reveals the intangible. In a sense, they trade the tangible for the intangible, seeking deeper truths hidden beneath the surface. They critically evaluate evidence, discerning what is valid, and once they have determined the truth, they defend it with unwavering conviction. This is their strength.

Like the Holy Spirit, straw builders seek wisdom and apply it with meticulous care. Yet this gift comes with a danger: if they choose the wrong source of knowledge, they may be led astray. Without remaining closely attuned to the whispers of the Spirit, they risk embracing falsehoods and falling into the wolf's grasp.

The Still Small Voice of the Straw

In divine innocence, the straw builder's connection to the Holy Spirit is expressed through a soft, quiet voice that carries an innate ability to calm and soothe. However, this gentle way of speaking can also cause the straw builder to perceive loud or boisterous voices as grating and overwhelming.

While the straw's voice is soft and calm, it is far from insignificant. Rooted in divine innocence, the straw builder's speech is often commanding in its clarity and precision. Their words are carefully measured, each one chosen with intention and thoughtfulness. This deliberate use of language reflects their intelligence and their deep understanding of life's complexities. The innocent straw builder often possesses an impressive memory and the ability to recall detailed information, yet they wield this skill humbly, never using it to boast or elevate themselves.

The straw builder is uniquely attuned to the wisdom and guidance of the Holy Spirit, often embodying the Spirit's role as a Comforter and Helper. As Jesus promised before His ascension, "And I will pray the Father, and he shall give you another Comforter, that he may abide with you for ever" (John 14:16). Like all builder types, the straw is blessed with the fruits of the Spirit: love, joy, peace, patience, kindness, goodness, faithfulness, gentleness, and self-control. Yet, for the straw builder, these gifts are uniquely channeled through their drive to help, comfort, and understand others.

However, this deep connection to the Spirit comes with its challenges. Without a strong faith in God to anchor them, the straw builder's heightened sensitivity can become a burden. The unbelieving or undisciplined straw may struggle to cope with the Spirit's discernment, which often makes them acutely aware of the world's suffering and injustices. In an attempt to dull this overwhelming sensitivity, they might turn to distractions such as substance abuse, video games, social media, or even compulsive learning. These behaviors serve as an escape from the weight of their gift, which they may not yet fully understand or appreciate.

In addition, a straw builder disconnected from divine innocence can become vulnerable to manipulation. Wolves may exploit their intelligence and sensitivity, shaping their perceptions with unrelenting falsehoods and using their gifts against them. This is why it is vital for the straw builder to remain grounded in their faith and aligned with their divine innocence.

When the straw builder embraces their divine innocence, they recognize that their gifts are not burdens but blessings meant to be shared. Their connection to the Holy Spirit becomes a source of strength and purpose, enabling them to act as a helper and comforter in service to others. In doing so, they express the Spirit's love, joy, peace, patience, kindness, goodness, faithfulness, gentleness, and self-control, becoming a living reflection of God's grace in the world.

QUIZ

ARE YOU A STRAW BUILDER?

In this section, you will have the opportunity to take a quiz to determine if you are a straw builder. This quiz is designed to separate the straw builder from other types by honing in on the core traits of the brick. Remember the caveat that we shared in the former builder chapters: it is possible to score as a straw builder when one is actually another type if one is living inauthentically (outside of one's divine innocence).

Reflect on each of the questions below, and answer each using the following scale:

1 Never

2 Rarely

3 Sometimes

4 Often

5 Always

1. Do you find detailed information interesting?

   1 - 2 - 3 - 4 - 5

2. If you had to relate to God the Father, Son, or Holy Spirit, would you choose the Holy Spirit?

   1 - 2 - 3 - 4 - 5

3. Do you respond best to soft, calming voices?

    1 - 2 - 3 - 4 - 5

4. When you were in school, were you only motivated to complete homework if you found it interesting or important?

    1 - 2 - 3 - 4 - 5

5. Do you enjoy discovering techniques that make work faster and easier?

    1 - 2 - 3 - 4 - 5

6. Does information need to be detailed and verifiable before you consider it valid?

    1 - 2 - 3 - 4 - 5

7. Do you enjoy the use of big or unfamiliar words?

    1 - 2 - 3 - 4 - 5

8. Do you prefer when others make decisions for you or assist you in decision-making?

    1 - 2 - 3 - 4 - 5

9. Do you believe it is possible to learn valuable lessons from people who lack the credentials critical to the subject?

    1 - 2 - 3 - 4 - 5

10. Do you spend significant time each week researching new concepts and topics?

    1 - 2 - 3 - 4 - 5

11. Are you skeptical of information that is not backed by concrete facts or authority?

    1 - 2 - 3 - 4 - 5

12. Do you view money primarily as a tool for gaining security?

    1 - 2 - 3 - 4 - 5

13. Do you prefer delegating responsibilities to others instead of handling them yourself?

    1 - 2 - 3 - 4 - 5

14. Do you tend to have a hands-off, laissez-faire management style?

    1 - 2 - 3 - 4 - 5

15. Do you think making your bed is a waste of time?

    1 - 2 - 3 - 4 - 5

16. Do you dismiss criticism easily and feel indignant when people question your knowledge?

    1 - 2 - 3 - 4 - 5

17. When you meet someone, do you observe them for the purpose of simply learning more about them?

    1 - 2 - 3 - 4 - 5

18. Are you quick and precise in getting to the point in a conversation?

    1 - 2 - 3 - 4 - 5

19. Do you often cry or become emotional over sad stories?

    1 - 2 - 3 - 4 - 5

20. Do you cringe when others see you as a pauper?

    1 - 2 - 3 - 4 - 5

21. Are you often told that you speak softly?

   1 - 2 - 3 - 4 - 5

How to Score Your Quiz:

If your score is between 84-105 you are most likely a straw builder living in your divine innocence. If your score was less than 84, you are most likely a different builder type.

Are You a Straw Builder Acting as the Wolf?

If your score indicates that you are a straw builder, take this quiz to determine the extent to which you are either living in innocence as the pig or ignorance as the wolf. If you are certain that you are a different type, skip this quiz and go to the next chapter.

Reflect on each of the questions below, and answer each using the following scale:

    1 Never

    2 Rarely

    3 Sometimes

    4 Often

    5 Always

1. Do you prefer to spend your time idly loitering or lingering without purpose?

   1 - 2 - 3 - 4 - 5

2. Do you insist on having time for fun no matter what is happening?

   1 - 2 - 3 - 4 - 5

3. In social or professional situations, do you frequently mention important or accomplished people to enhance your own status?

   1 - 2 - 3 - 4 - 5

4. When you are completely honest with yourself, do you enjoy talking about famous or influential people, especially if you are connected to them?

   1 - 2 - 3 - 4 - 5

5. Do you feel the need to seek permission from an authority figure before you can confidently move forward?

   1 - 2 - 3 - 4 - 5

6. Do you feel confident that you are "in the know"?

   1 - 2 - 3 - 4 - 5

7. Are you often impatient with others or with yourself?

   1 - 2 - 3 - 4 - 5

8. Do you strongly believe that your chosen source of information is completely factual while dismissing others as entirely false?

   1 - 2 - 3 - 4 - 5

9. Have you ever experienced analysis paralysis, where you are unable to make a decision due to overanalyzing information?

1 - 2 - 3 - 4 - 5

10. Do you value play over work?

1 - 2 - 3 - 4 - 5

11. Do you consider yourself an expert?

1 - 2 - 3 - 4 - 5

12. When you are against someone, do you belittle them?

1 - 2 - 3 - 4 - 5

How to Score the Quiz:

The Wolf: A score between 48-60 indicates more wolf-like tendencies and ignorance of your actions. You are most certainly living as the wolf if you scored in this range.

The Pig: A score between 24-47 indicates that you are living in divine innocence most of the time. Your lower score shows that you have greater awareness and commitment to living in innocence. You are aware of your behavior and are striving toward divine innocence. Like the rest of us, you do not always succeed but you recognize when you are being the wolf.

The Wolf in Disguise: A score between 12-23 likely indicates that you are in denial about your wolfish tendencies and are likely acting as the wolf in ways that you are unaware of. You are the wolf in disguise, as the wolf who dressed as grandma in Little Red Riding Hood. The "never" response is most significant—if you consistently claim to never engage in wolfish behavior, it may indicate denial or an inability to recognize your own actions.

If you scored above 44 or under 22 on this quiz, take some time to self-reflect and seek your holy innocence through prayer and study. In this way, you can find your way back to your divine innocence and live joyfully and peacefully as your true builder type. If you feel certain that you are a stick builder, implement the techniques we have shown you here to return to innocence.

CHAPTER 6

THE WOLF

The Wolf Within

When I was young, I dreamed of being a teacher. I wanted to be just like Mrs. Patterson, my high school math teacher. She was so encouraging and made learning feel exciting. But that dream never came to be. I was the only son my father never had, and the family business needed me. The lure of responsibility and legacy pulled me in. At first, I earned nothing but a meager salary, but I saw the potential. If I worked strategically and climbed the ladder to become a manager, I could earn more. And if I made it to CEO, I could finally be in charge.

I believed, wholeheartedly, that I could run the company better than anyone else. To me, the business was plagued by incompetence. People mismanaged funds, resources, and opportunities. So many had embezzled from us over the years. My father, however, had a different perspective. He believed the people who were loyal to us—our long-standing employees—were the ones who had saved the business. I didn't share his faith. When I became CEO, I fired everyone. I thought we needed a clean slate, a fresh start to eliminate all the weaknesses that had been holding us back.

I married young, with innocence and hope for the future, but that turned out to be one of my greatest mistakes. My husband was a disappointment from the start—a good-for-nothing dreamer who never worked hard enough, never accomplished anything meaningful, and never listened to me.

When we first met, I thought he was sweet and had potential. I believed I could help him become a better man. He was a mechanic back then, with big dreams that I supported. His mother had treated him terribly, leaving him insecure and unsure of his worth. I thought, naively, that with my encouragement, he would grow stronger, more capable. Instead, he decided to quit his job and pursue a career as a massage therapist.

Can you imagine? A mechanic turning into a massage therapist? It was absurd. Most of his clients would obviously be women. I couldn't help but wonder why he made such a choice. Did he want to touch other women? He swore to me he never cheated, but I could never fully trust him again.

Our marriage was a series of separations and reconciliations. I tried so hard to make it work. I gave it my all. I even had two children with him, thinking it might bring us closer. But in the end, he was impossible to live with. Even now, being around him is unbearable.

236

The kids are grown now, but whenever there's a family gathering, I make sure to arrive at a different time than him. I can't stand being in the same room with him. It's too traumatic. The children honor my request, and while I'm grateful, it doesn't make it any easier.

When we divorced, I made sure I got what I deserved. I was the one with the money. His car repair shop, which later became a massage parlor, was essentially funded by me anyway. The law in our state said he was entitled to half, but I wasn't about to let that happen. I played the long game, and in the end, I kept 90% of what was mine. I'm proud of that.

I thought for sure he would fail without me. I was certain that his business would crumble. Yet somehow, it hasn't. His massage parlor is thriving, and he seems to be paying his bills. I'm still convinced he's teetering on the edge of bankruptcy, but for now, he's made it work. I suppose I should be happy for him, but honestly, I don't give it much thought anymore.

As for me, I'm still running my business. I'm growing, expanding, and thriving in ways I always knew I could. Just last week, the local newspaper came to cover one of our events. It was a great moment of recognition for all we're doing in the community.

But it is not all smooth sailing. Finding good help is a constant battle. Most people, in my experience, are lazy and lack intelligence. I wish I could say otherwise, but it's the truth. Managing employees is one of the hardest parts of my job, but I persevere. I soldier on because

I love my kids, and I believe God is pleased with me, even if no one else truly understands me.

How the Wolf Sees the World

Every one of us has the capacity to live in divine innocence as a stick, straw, or brick pig, or in ignorance as the wolf. It is likely that we all recognize a bit of ourselves in the allegory above. This is normal. The important thing is to acknowledge how the wolf manifests in us and to seek a way back to divine innocence. That is the purpose of this chapter: to explore the characteristics of the wolf and how they apply to all builder types.

As you read, we encourage you to focus on how the wolf shows up in you rather than how it appears in others. Introspection is key to recognizing the wolf within. If you are concerned about others, you can always recommend that they read this book for themselves. As the saying goes, "Stay in your lane." Or, to frame it within this allegory, stay in your own house and resist the urge to huff and puff in front of someone else's door.

Denial and Projection

One of the quintessential wolfish traits is the tendency to deny one's bad behavior while simultaneously calling out others for theirs. The wolf does not recognize its own actions, focusing instead on the behavior of others as a perceived threat to its survival. Deep down, the wolf believes life is a battle: hunt or be hunted. If they are not the predator, they fear becoming the prey.

This belief manifests in behaviors such as bullying. Wolves can be mean and dismissive without remorse or self-reflection. They may mock, taunt, or belittle others, sometimes subtly, but always in a way that reveals their inability to empathize or take responsibility for their actions. Even when presented with evidence of their wrongdoing, the wolf turns a blind eye, clinging to denial as a means of maintaining their perceived strength and power.

The wolf refuses to admit its faults because doing so feels like weakness. Restoring or resolving the harm they have caused is rarely an option, as the thought of returning to innocence—a vulnerable state —feels unbearable. Instead, the wolf fortifies its ignorance, leaving victims emotionally scarred and mentally wounded. In extreme cases, physical abuse may also occur, further devastating the victim's connection to their own innocence. Tragically, these experiences can lead the victim to adopt wolf-like behaviors, perpetuating the cycle of ignorance and harm.

Abandoning the Home of Innocence

Why would someone abandon their divine innocence? When the wolf invades our home, huffing and puffing until it collapses, the devastation can feel irreparable. In those moments, it seems easier to leave the ruins behind and search for a new home. What we fail to understand is that there is no other home. The home of our divine innocence is the only true dwelling for our soul, and though it may lie in ruins, it can always be rebuilt.

Rebuilding this home requires staying true to our divine innocence, even when it feels difficult. It demands trust in our true selves and faith that our efforts will sustain us through the process. In the end, the home can be restored stronger than before, capable of withstanding future attacks.

The Burden of the Wolf

The wolf carries a heavy, unacknowledged burden: the pain of leaving the home of innocence. This deep, existential wound drives much of the wolf's behavior, yet it remains hidden even from themselves. Instead of facing this pain, the wolf projects it outward, blaming others for the very attitudes and actions they themselves exhibit.

For example, a wolf who hides things from their spouse may accuse their spouse of deceit. They project their own behavior onto others, genuinely believing the accusations. This phenomenon, while baffling to outsiders, is entirely unconscious for the wolf. They cannot see their own guilt or its projection, creating a cycle of ignorance that feeds on itself.

This denial defines the wolf's ignorance. They avoid or ignore truths that are plain to others, replacing them with lies or misrepresentations that preserve their distorted self-image. The wolf deceives not only others but also themselves, using this strategy to avoid the turmoil caused by their separation from innocence.

The Wolf's Anger and Manipulation

The wolf's anger often stems from their perception of others' actions as threats. This anger, combined with their manipulative tendencies, leads them to attack those who embody innocence. The wolf's huffing and puffing—whether through harsh words, spiteful actions, or emotional manipulation—creates chaos for their victims.

To those living in divine innocence, the wolf's attacks feel like an assault on their natural perception of the world. For other wolves, these attacks can spark a conflict that spirals into an unwinnable war. The wolf's actions do not lead to resolution or peace; they deepen the divide between themselves and the world around them.

Breaking the Cycle

Understanding how the wolf operates within us is the first step toward breaking free from its influence. The wolf's ignorance blinds us to the truth of who we are and the harm we cause. By recognizing these patterns, we can begin the process of rebuilding the home of our divine innocence, reconnecting with the truth of our souls, and finding peace within ourselves.

In the end, the wolf is not an external enemy. It is the part of us that has lost its way, that believes strength lies in denial and aggression rather than vulnerability and truth. To overcome the wolf, we must return to the foundation of our innocence, trusting that it is strong enough to rebuild and endure.

How the Wolf Acts in the World

Recognizing the wolf—whether it is within ourselves or in others—is critical. In this section, we will examine the wolf's typical behaviors and characteristics to help identify and understand them.

Denial and Self-Deception

The wolf begins by deceiving itself, believing it is righteous no matter its actions or the evidence to the contrary. Consider a housekeeper at a five-star hotel who is told that guests complained about hair in the shower of a recently cleaned room. A wolfish housekeeper would adamantly deny the claim, accusing the guests of lying or exaggerating. They might clean the next room more thoroughly, but only to avoid further criticism, and they would never reflect on the original mistake. Eventually, this pattern of denial would cost them their job, and they would complain that no one gave them a fair chance.

By contrast, an innocent housekeeper would apologize immediately, take responsibility for the oversight, and commit to being more attentive in the future. Their honesty and willingness to improve would earn the respect of their manager and strengthen their workplace relationships.

Superiority and Projection

The wolf sees itself as superior to everyone else—smarter, more competent, and more deserving of respect. This arrogance often manifests in dismissive language, like calling others "stupid" or "annoying." It may even appear in subtler ways, such as wearing a t-shirt with slogans like "I like my cats and maybe three people" or "I like coffee and sunsets…you, not so much." These behaviors, while seemingly humorous, are forms of name-calling that reinforce the wolf's belief in its own superiority.

Another hallmark of the wolf is labeling others as "toxic." Ironically, the wolf is often the most toxic of all. The term "toxic" itself can be seen as a wolfish invention, a derogatory label meant to elevate the speaker above those they deem unworthy. The innocent mind, by contrast, does not divide people into categories of "toxic" and "non-toxic." Instead, it simply decides who to associate with and who to avoid, without resorting to divisive language or judgments.

When the innocent pig encounters a wolf, they do not waste time analyzing the wolf's behavior or motivations. They focus instead on protecting themselves by keeping the wolf outside their house. The innocent pig does not engage in the wolf's game of manipulation or division; they preserve their energy and attention for what truly matters—maintaining their own divine innocence.

Projection as a Defense Mechanism

Projection is one of the wolf's most consistent behaviors. Modern psychology defines projection as attributing one's own thoughts, feelings, or behaviors to others. The wolf cries wolf, accusing others of the very actions or attitudes they themselves embody. For instance, a wolf who lies habitually will accuse others of dishonesty, or a wolf who cheats in a relationship will become obsessed with the idea that their partner is unfaithful.

Projection allows the wolf to avoid the painful truths about themselves by transferring those truths onto others. This is a defense mechanism designed to preserve their self-image. However, it does not quench the underlying fire of guilt, shame, or remorse. Instead, the wolf's inner turmoil remains, burning endlessly until they confront the truth. The act of projection may provide temporary relief, but it deepens their ignorance and reinforces their wolfish behavior.

Endless Competition

The wolf is consumed by competition. Their interactions with others are often defined by a constant need to dominate, manipulate, and win. For the wolf, life is a zero-sum game—someone must lose for them to win. This mindset poisons their relationships and prevents them from experiencing true joy or fulfillment.

The innocent pig, by contrast, may compete for fun, personal growth, or even to glorify God, but they do not measure their worth or

244

the worth of others by the outcome of these competitions. They see value in the process itself, not just the results. The wolf, however, equates winning with superiority and losing with failure. If the wolf cannot win fairly, they will resort to name-calling, sabotage, or playing the victim to undermine their competitors.

In some cases, the wolf will champion the cause of the underdog—not out of genuine concern, but as a way to position themselves as virtuous while attacking the perceived "winners." This behavior is not born of compassion but of bitterness and envy.

Abusing Power

The wolf is an abuser of power, no matter how much or how little they possess. Their actions are motivated by self-interest, often at the expense of others. Consider the story of a drunk driver who caused a fatal accident involving a couple on their way to church. Trapped in her car, the driver screamed for help, demanding attention for her own injuries while ignoring the devastating consequences of her actions. This self-centeredness is quintessentially wolfish—using one's power, whether it be the power of a vehicle, a position of authority, or physical strength, solely for personal gain without regard for others.

Transforming Tragedy into Strength

The interaction between the wolf and the innocent pig can be devastating, but it also presents an opportunity for growth. When the wolf blows down the pig's house, it forces the pig to rebuild. If the innocent pig learns from the experience, they will construct a stronger, more resilient house. This process of rebuilding is not just about physical or external structures—it is about reinforcing their connection to divine innocence.

The wolf's intention is always to destroy, but their actions can unintentionally strengthen the innocent who remain vigilant and refuse to succumb to wolfish behavior. This is why it is crucial to recognize the wolf within ourselves and others, not to condemn or judge, but to ensure that we stay true to our divine nature.

> *"The wolf's intention is always to destroy, but their actions can unintentionally strengthen the innocent who remain vigilant."*

The Wolf's Impact on Society

The wolf's behavior extends beyond individual interactions to influence larger systems and institutions. Businesses, organizations, religions, and even scientific endeavors can become wolfish when they prioritize self-interest, manipulation, and division over truth, integrity, and service. For instance, when science is manipulated for profit or propaganda, it strays from its purpose of discovery and truth-seeking. Similarly, when religious institutions focus on power and control rather than spiritual growth, they lose their connection to divine innocence.

Recognizing the wolf's presence in these systems requires the same vigilance we apply to our personal lives. We must hold ourselves and our institutions accountable, ensuring that they operate in alignment with divine principles rather than wolfish ignorance. Only then can we create a world where innocence, wisdom, and compassion prevail over manipulation, competition, and destruction.

By identifying and addressing the wolfish tendencies within ourselves and the systems we interact with, we take an essential step toward restoring our divine innocence and living in harmony with others.

Understanding the Wolf in Us Empowers Us to Change

Before we begin, we want to be clear: you cannot change the wolf in others. You can only change the wolf within yourself. As you read this section, we encourage you to focus on how the wolf operates in you rather than in those around you. The wolf's intention is always to destroy, but their actions can unintentionally strengthen the innocent who remain vigilant.

"You cannot change the wolf in others. You can only change the wolf within yourself."

It is human nature to deflect and project. We have all been there—listening to advice or a motivational talk and thinking, "Oh, I wish so-and-so could hear this." In that moment, we stop seeking our own growth and focus on how others should change. This is why we ask you to look inward. Remember the old adage: when you point a finger at someone else, three fingers point back at you. Instead of pointing outward, let's focus on ourselves and work toward becoming the best versions of who we are meant to be.

Choosing Innocence Over Chaos

Understanding how the wolf operates equips us to choose innocence over ignorance. But this choice is not easy. It is human nature to gravitate toward chaos, which feels tangible and predictable, rather than to trust in the intangible and often uncomfortable path of innocence. We focus on the wolf huffing and puffing at the door instead of trusting in the strength of the walls that protect us. If we give in to fear, we open the door to fight the wolf or escape through a back window, running to a neighbor's house and huffing and puffing at their door. Either way, the wolf consumes us, turning us into its prey.

When the wolf shows up, the signs are unmistakable. The wolf lacks remorse, avoids self-reflection, and fixates on others' perceived faults while remaining blind to its own. Wolves treat others as obstacles or tools rather than as valuable individuals deserving of love and support. To the wolf, the problem is always the other person—never themselves.

Faith in Divine Innocence

When faced with conflict, our instinct is seldom to stay rooted in innocence. Why? Because we doubt its strength. We fail to see that our innocence, when aligned with the divine, is more than enough to sustain us. On its own, our innocence feels fragile, but in partnership with the divine, it is unassailable. There is no such thing as innocence apart from the divine. True innocence is inherently divine and comes with the full protection of that connection.

To remain in divine innocence when the wolf is threatening, we must trust that we are not alone. Our homes—our inner selves—are built with walls strong enough to withstand the wolf's attacks, but we must have faith in that truth. Faith requires action. It calls us to stand firm, trusting in the divine strength that fortifies us. This choice allows us to transcend the chaos of the wolf and remain untouched by its influence.

A Personal Encounter with the Wolf

When the wolf came to my door recently, I (Robert) felt overwhelmed by fear and panic. My initial instincts were to fight or flee. I wrestled with the decision: should I open the door and face the wolf head-on, or should I run to my neighbor's house for help, inadvertently bringing chaos to their door? Both options seemed plausible in the heat of the moment, but both would have led to the same outcome: I would have become the wolf.

A trusted friend offered wise counsel, reminding me of the strength of my home and the divine power that protects it. I chose to remain where I was, allowing the wolf to huff and puff without engaging. This act of faith transformed my fear into peace. The wolf's noise became powerless against the divine strength within me.

I realized that my only job was to trust the illuminated path before me. It was not my responsibility to see the full picture or control every outcome—that is God's role. When we try to control the future, we invite the wolf into our lives. Trusting the divine means taking one step at a time, confident that the divine has plans to prosper us, not to harm us.

The Scriptures offered me great comfort during this time. Two verses, in particular, resonated with me:

> "For thou art my lamp, O Lord: and the Lord will lighten my darkness" (2 Samuel 22:29 KJV).

> "For I know the plans I have for you," says the Lord, "plans to prosper you and not to harm you, to give you a future and a hope" (Jeremiah 29:11 NIV).

These verses reminded me to focus on God's guidance and find peace in my divine innocence, trusting that all things would work together for good.

Opposition as Opportunity

Another way the wolf manifests is through our fear of opposing perspectives. It is natural to feel threatened by viewpoints that challenge our own, especially when we have worked hard to build our lives and achieve our goals. Opposition can feel like a destabilizing force, a wrench in our carefully laid plans. Yet this fear is rooted in fallacy. Opposition is not inherently wolfish. Instead, it offers a valuable opportunity to grow.

Engaging with opposing views can expand our understanding, challenge our biases, and strengthen our beliefs. When we approach these situations with an open mind, we distinguish facts from fear or misinformation, allowing divine innocence to guide our decisions. Opposition, when embraced with humility and curiosity, becomes a pathway to wisdom.

Breaking the Chain of Chaos

The wolf thrives on chaos, creating chain reactions of fear, anger, and division. When one person succumbs to the wolf, their actions ripple outward, affecting everyone around them. However, innocence has the power to create a different kind of chain reaction. By staying rooted in divine innocence, even in the face of the wolf's attacks, we inspire others to do the same. This ripple effect of peace and strength can counteract the wolf's chaos.

The key to resisting the wolf lies in trust—trust in the divine and in the strength of the home we have built. By refusing to engage with the wolf on its terms, we protect our innocence and foster a world where light and truth prevail. When we focus on the path illuminated before us, taking one faithful step at a time, we empower ourselves to live in divine innocence and inspire others to do the same.

The Speed of Transformation and the Need for Vigilance

The speed with which peace can dissolve into chaos at the presence of just one wolf is a sobering reminder of the importance of constant vigilance. While we all crave a peaceful and harmonious environment, achieving and maintaining such an atmosphere requires effort and awareness. It demands that we always remain prepared to confront the wolf, whether it emerges in others or within ourselves, and to do so in a way that is firmly rooted in divine innocence. A semi-orderly society governed by law and order helps to keep the wolf at bay by countering the destructive tendencies in human nature. Even simple acts of love, devotion, and genuine care for the sanctity of life act as powerful deterrents to the wolf's influence. Very often, combating the wolf isn't any more complicated than that.

As previously discussed, recognizing the wolf in others is much easier than identifying it in ourselves. Admitting that we have been the wolf takes courage, honesty, and humility. It's not just pride or a refusal to admit fault that hinders us, but also the wolf's inherent ignorance. By definition, the wolf does not recognize himself as such. Sometimes, the wolf isn't merely huffing and puffing outside our door —he's already inside. Looking in the mirror and being willing to confront what we see can reveal the wolf lurking within. This wolf may not have visible fangs, claws, or fur, but he is there, often disguised in ways that make him hard to detect.

Letting the Wolf In

We might have allowed the wolf into our souls without even realizing it, simply by neglecting our innocence. Perhaps worse, we might have opened the door to the wolf through the influence of social conditioning, toxic environments, or the consumption of depravity in media, television, or social platforms. What we watch, listen to, and internalize matters deeply. Ideas introduced through social movements often evolve into widespread beliefs, which in turn shape societal norms. Without even realizing it, these external forces can grant the wolf entry into our minds and hearts.

The Wolf's Blindness

Without divine intervention, the wolf remains the wolf. Ignorant of his true nature, the wolf cannot see his own flaws and refuses to consider that there is anything wrong with him. Instead of seeking divine innocence, he doubles down on his wolfish behaviors. Isolating himself from those who might hold up a mirror to his actions, the wolf gravitates toward other wolves or toward pigs who are willing to believe his stories. He reframes his narrative, casting himself as both victim and victor. In contrast, someone rooted in divine innocence can identify the wolfish behaviors within themselves and pull themselves back from the brink. This ability to self-reflect and correct course is one of the key differences between living in divine innocence and succumbing to the wolf within. Recognizing wolfish tendencies allows us to stop, reassess, and consciously choose a better path, while the ignorant wolf remains trapped in a cycle of self-deception and destruction.

Renouncing the Wolf in Our Souls

This brings us to the crucial question: how do we renounce the wolf? The first step is simple, yet profoundly challenging: we must recognize the wolf within ourselves. The moment we admit that we have been the "bad guy," we take the first step toward reclaiming our innocence. However, this recognition is not something we can achieve alone. By nature, ignorance blinds us to our own faults. To see what we cannot see on

> *"Any friendship, any relationship, or any marriage can succeed when too different builder groups remain in their divining innocence."*

our own, we must ask for divine help. This requires humility, honesty, and a willingness to be wrong.

The only way to truly expose the wolf in us is to pray for the ability to see it. We must ask God to reveal any ignorance, selfishness, or destructive tendencies within us. This is not about attending church or performing religious rituals—it is about developing a personal and authentic relationship with God as we understand Him. It is about focusing inward, seeking divine guidance, and opening ourselves to the possibility of transformation.

Why is a relationship with God essential in this process? The answer lies in the nature of our ignorance. If something is not part of our perceptual field, we cannot address it. Even if others point out our flaws, we may remain blind to them unless we are spiritually prepared to see them. It is through prayer and divine intervention that these blind spots can be illuminated. This is why humility and a willingness to change are critical. Without them, we remain trapped in the wolf's ignorance, unable to move toward innocence.

Twelve Steps to Return to Divine Innocence

In reflecting on this journey, we have found the principles of the twelve-step recovery process to be remarkably applicable to renouncing the wolf and embracing divine innocence. It began, as most of us know, as an addiction treatment system under the name Alcoholics Anonymous. We give them tremendous credit. In my view, its steps are a flexible and powerful foundation for transformation. These steps provide a clear and practical framework for moving from ignorance to awareness, from selfishness to selflessness, and from wolfishness to innocence.

Step 1: Honesty
Admit that we are powerless over the wolf within us and that our lives have become unmanageable.

One of the defining traits of the wolf is his refusal to take responsibility for his actions. He shifts blame, denies his faults, and stubbornly clings to the belief that he is always in the right. This unyielding arrogance keeps the wolf trapped in ignorance and separates him from divine innocence. To return to innocence, we must first be willing to humble ourselves and acknowledge where we have gone wrong. This step requires courage and vulnerability, as it involves confronting truths about ourselves that we may not want to face.

The path back to innocence begins with a simple but profound act: admitting that we need help. This is where divine intervention, as mentioned earlier, becomes essential. However, divine help can only work in our lives if we are willing to accept it. This willingness starts with the recognition of our limitations, an acknowledgment that we have made mistakes and cannot solve everything on our own.

The most wolfish statement a person can utter is, "I know." These words are a shield the wolf uses to defend his ego, closing himself off to growth and wisdom. By contrast, the most innocent words we can say are, "I may be wrong." This statement reflects humility, openness, and a willingness to learn. It is a declaration that we do not have all the answers and that we are open to guidance. It is the first step in laying down the heavy burden of arrogance and embracing the freedom that comes with humility.

When we say, "I may be wrong," we create space for change. We allow ourselves to be taught, corrected, and guided toward a better path. This simple admission disarms the wolf within us, replacing his huffing and puffing with a quiet, steadfast faith in the process of transformation. By accepting that we are not infallible, we pave the way for divine innocence to take its rightful place at the center of our lives.

Step 2: Hope

Believe that a power greater than ourselves can restore us to innocence.

Hope is the lifeblood of transformation. It is the quiet assurance that no matter how far we have wandered from the path of divine innocence, there is always a way back. This hope, however, must be genuine. The wolf's version of hope is an illusion—a mirage that offers temporary comfort but no true direction. The wolf places his hope in external sources: his own cunning, power, or the validation of others. Yet these are fleeting and unreliable, leading only to deeper dissatisfaction.

True hope, by contrast, is rooted in something greater than ourselves. It is the belief that there is a divine force—a Power beyond human understanding—that is both willing and able to guide us back to innocence. This hope is not wishful thinking; it is a profound trust in the goodness and wisdom of that higher Power. It is the assurance that our mistakes, no matter how severe, do not define us and that redemption is always possible.

To embrace this step, we must release the false hope that the wolf clings to and replace it with a hope grounded in faith. This shift is transformative. Instead of relying on our limited strength and knowledge, we surrender to the guidance of the divine. Hope becomes the bridge that connects us to the possibility of change, lighting the path forward when all else seems dark.

Without true hope, it is nearly impossible to find or even believe in the innocence within us. But when we choose to hope in something greater, we begin to see that our divine innocence has never truly left us. It has been waiting patiently for us to return, and through this hope, we take the first steps toward reclaiming it.

Step 3: Faith
Decide to turn our will and lives over to the care of God as we understand Him

Faith is the bridge between hope and transformation. It is the act of believing in what cannot be seen, touched, or fully comprehended, yet trusting in its truth and power. In this step, we take a profound leap of faith by surrendering control of our lives to God, as we understand Him. This is not a passive resignation but an active decision to let go of the reins we have held so tightly and place them in divine hands.

To turn our will and lives over to God is an act of profound humility. It is an acknowledgment that our own understanding and efforts have not been enough to lead us to the peace and innocence we seek. Faith does not require us to know what God will do or how He will do it. Instead, it asks us to trust that whatever God allows into our lives is part of a greater plan for our highest good.

This surrender can feel frightening at first. The wolf within us clings to control, convinced that letting go is a sign of weakness or defeat. But in truth, it is through surrender that we discover strength. By releasing our grip on the need to control every outcome, we create space for divine wisdom to guide us.

Faith is not blind; it is illuminated by the knowledge that God is good and that His care for us is steadfast and unchanging. It is the belief that He sees the path ahead even when we cannot and that He is leading us toward a life of divine innocence and peace.

Through this act of faith, we realign our lives with a higher purpose. We begin to let go of the wolf's illusions of self-reliance and control, replacing them with trust in the divine. This trust allows us to rest in the assurance that God is not only able to lead us but is also eager to restore us to the innocence we were created to embody. Faith becomes the turning point where we stop striving to fix ourselves and start allowing God to transform us from within.

Step 4: Courage
Conduct a fearless and honest moral inventory of ourselves.

This step calls for bravery of the highest order. It is not a surface-level reflection or a passing glance at our actions; it is a searching and fearless moral inventory, a deep dive into the ways we have acted as the wolf in our lives. To do this, we must summon courage—the kind of courage that allows us to face uncomfortable truths about ourselves without turning away.

We cannot accomplish this step on our own. The wolf, by its very nature, is blind to its own faults. The wolf cannot see the truth about itself, because its ignorance serves as a shield against the discomfort of self-awareness. This is why we must turn to God for guidance during this process. Only through divine illumination can we begin to recognize the wolf within us and the ways it has manifested in our relationships, choices, and behaviors.

Courage in this step is not just the willingness to see our faults; it is also the willingness to accept them. It requires us to be honest without excuses, defenses, or justifications. It means acknowledging not only what we have done but also why we have done it, understanding how the wolf's influence has shaped our actions.

The process of taking this inventory is deeply humbling. It strips away the illusions we have created about ourselves, the stories we have told to avoid responsibility. But in this humility lies the seed of transformation. By naming and confronting the wolf within, we begin to loosen its grip on our lives.

This step is not about self-condemnation; it is about self-awareness. It is not about dwelling in guilt or shame but about opening the door to healing and change. With God's help, we can examine our lives with honesty and compassion, recognizing our mistakes without losing sight of our worth.

Through this fearless moral inventory, we take a crucial step toward reclaiming our innocence. We acknowledge the truth about ourselves, and in doing so, we prepare the ground for the divine to work in us, restoring us to the people we were created to be. Courage becomes the key that unlocks the door to redemption and renewal.

Step 5: Integrity
Admit to God, to ourselves, and to another human being the exact nature of our wrongs.

Integrity begins with honesty, and in this step, we take the profound and humbling action of admitting the exact nature of our wolfish behavior. This admission is not just a passing acknowledgment but a deliberate act of confession. We bring our wrongs into the light— before God, before ourselves, and before another trusted person— allowing the truth to break through the walls of ignorance and denial that the wolf has built around us.

Someone once said that the two most powerful statements in the human experience are "I love you" and "I'm sorry." These words are bridges that reconnect us to others and to our true selves. They carry the potential for healing, for hope, and for transformation. When spoken to God, they take on an even deeper significance. "I'm sorry" becomes a surrender, an acknowledgment of our limitations and our need for divine grace. "I love you" becomes an expression of our desire to return to the innocence that God has placed within us.

A personal example illustrates this step perfectly. As we were writing this chapter, my editor shared a deeply reflective thought with me. She admitted that in her life, there were times when she was the villain in other people's stories. Sometimes this was due to their misinterpretation of her actions, but sometimes, she said, it was because of her own wolfish behavior. This honest recognition of the impact her actions had on others, even when painful, was a powerful step toward reclaiming her innocence.

This step requires a willingness to confront not only our actions but also the motivations behind them. It calls us to look at how the wolf has operated in our lives and to share that truth openly, first with God, then with ourselves, and finally with another human being. This final element—confessing to another person—helps to break the isolation that the wolf thrives on. It invites accountability and restores connection.

Admitting our wrongs is a deeply vulnerable act, but it is through vulnerability that we find strength. In naming our faults, we begin to dissolve the power that secrecy and denial hold over us. We let go of the shame that keeps us trapped, and we allow ourselves to be seen, both by others and by the divine, as we truly are.

In this step, we come back into alignment with our divine nature. Integrity is not about perfection; it is about living in truth. By admitting the exact nature of our wrongs, we take another crucial step toward innocence, clearing the path for healing, reconciliation, and growth. This is the beginning of restoration, where the weight of our wolfish behavior is lifted, and we are free to walk in the light of who we are meant to be.

Step 6: Willingness

Become entirely ready to have God remove all our defects of character

In this step, we prepare our hearts and minds to release the wolfish habits that have driven us away from the home of our divine innocence. It is not enough to simply recognize the wolf within us. Recognition without action keeps us trapped in the same patterns of thought and behavior. We must reach the point of being entirely ready —ready to let go of our reliance on the wolf and trust God to guide us back to our true selves.

This willingness is pivotal, because the wolf often masquerades as our protector, offering us a false sense of safety and control. The wolf's habits, though destructive, can feel familiar and even comforting, as they are built on patterns we've relied on for years to survive. Letting go of these behaviors can feel like stepping into the unknown, and for many of us, the unknown is terrifying. But it is only by becoming willing to surrender these habits that we create space for the divine to work in us and through us.

Consider this: when we are entrenched in wolfish behavior, we are clinging to strategies that once felt necessary, but now serve only to separate us from the divine. These behaviors may include self-criticism, judgment of others, manipulation, or even stubborn pride. In some way, we believe they are serving us—protecting us, making us stronger, or giving us power. But in truth, they are illusions, and they prevent us from experiencing the peace and freedom that come with divine innocence.

Becoming ready to have God remove these defects requires trust and courage. We must trust that God knows what is best for us, even when we cannot yet see it. We must trust that surrendering these wolfish habits will not leave us empty, but will instead create a fertile space for growth, healing, and love.

This step also requires humility. It is an acknowledgment that we cannot fix ourselves through sheer willpower. If we could have done it on our own, we would have done so already. Instead, we must turn to God and ask for His help. This willingness is not passive; it is an active choice to let go of the wolfish patterns that have defined us and to invite God into the process of transformation.

It is important to note that being willing does not mean being perfect. We will likely falter, and the wolf will try to creep back in. But each time we notice the wolf, we can return to this step, renewing our willingness to let go and let God work within us.

The act of becoming entirely ready is a profound shift in our perspective. It is the moment when we stop fighting to control our lives and start trusting in a higher power. It is the moment when we release our grip on the wolf and open our hands to receive the blessings of divine innocence.

This willingness marks a turning point in our journey. It is the bridge between recognizing the wolf and taking the steps to leave it behind. By embracing this readiness, we align ourselves with the divine and prepare to live as the people we were always meant to be: innocent, free, and whole.

Step 7: Humility
Humbly ask God to remove our shortcomings.

In this step, we come to God in prayer with an open heart, asking Him to remove the wolfishness that has taken root within us. This is not a casual request, but an act of profound humility and surrender. We acknowledge that we cannot transform ourselves through our own efforts, and we trust in God's power to lead us back to divine innocence.

To humbly ask God to remove our shortcomings is to recognize that we need His grace to overcome the ignorance that blinds us. The wolf thrives in the shadows of denial, distortion, and arrogance. By asking God to remove the veil from our eyes, we take a step toward the light of truth, a truth that only God can fully reveal to us.

This step is not about perfection or instant change. It is about opening ourselves to the process of divine transformation. We are not demanding that God fix us immediately; instead, we are surrendering to His timing and trusting in His plan. This act of humility shifts our focus away from our own efforts and toward God's infinite wisdom and power.

As we pray for God to remove our shortcomings, we must also be willing to let go of the illusions that have kept us tethered to the wolf. These illusions might include the belief that we are unworthy of love, that we must control everything to feel safe, or that we are defined by our mistakes. By humbly asking God for help, we acknowledge that these beliefs are false and that our true identity is found in His love and truth.

Humility is not weakness; it is strength rooted in surrender. When we ask God to remove our wolfishness, we are not admitting defeat but embracing the divine power that makes true transformation possible. We recognize that our safety, security, and sense of worth do not come from the wolf's illusions of control or dominance. Instead, they come from living in alignment with divine innocence—an innocence that reminds us we are truly safe, secure, loved, and capable of loving others.

This step also deepens our relationship with God. Through humility, we invite Him into the most vulnerable parts of our hearts, trusting that He will work within us to heal and restore. It is in this vulnerability that we find strength, for it is here that God meets us with His unwavering love and grace.

By humbly asking God to remove our shortcomings, we take an essential step on the path to wholeness. We acknowledge that we cannot do this alone, and we trust in the divine to lead us back to the truth of who we are. Through this act of humility, we begin to see the world—and ourselves—through the lens of divine innocence, and we take another step away from the wolf and toward the home of our soul.

Step 8: Love
Make a list of all persons we have harmed and become willing to make amends to them all.

The essence of this step is love—true, unconditional love that comes from divine innocence. One of the defining characteristics of the wolf is hatred, a destructive force that often masquerades as love. The wolf may deceive others—and even himself—into believing that his actions are rooted in love, but in reality, his love is conditional, manipulative, or self-serving. The wolf cannot truly love others because he does not even love himself.

In this step, we begin the process of shedding all forms of hatred, including the subtle yet pervasive self-hate that often hides beneath the wolf's bravado. To move toward divine innocence, we must recognize that true love cannot coexist with hatred or resentment, whether directed at ourselves or others. This is not an easy task, but it is essential for restoring harmony within ourselves and in our relationships.

We start by making a list of all the people we have harmed, whether intentionally or unintentionally. This requires deep self-reflection and honesty, as we confront the ways in which our wolfish behaviors have caused pain or damage. It is important to approach this step with humility, resisting the urge to justify or minimize our actions. Each name on the list is a reminder of the harm we have done and an opportunity to move toward restoration.

As we make our list, we also become willing to make amends to each person on it. This willingness is a crucial component of love. It requires us to let go of pride, fear, and excuses, and to embrace the possibility of healing and reconciliation. Being willing to make amends does not mean we will succeed in repairing every relationship or that every person will be receptive to our efforts. It means we are prepared to take responsibility for our actions and to do our part in seeking forgiveness and restoration.

At the heart of this step is the recognition that love is a transformative force. When we choose to love instead of hate, we align ourselves with divine innocence. This love is not a fleeting emotion or a superficial gesture; it is an active, deliberate choice to value others and to honor the divine within them. Love compels us to face the consequences of our actions, to take responsibility for the harm we have caused, and to seek ways to restore what has been broken.

Letting go of self-hate is equally important. We cannot fully love others if we do not love ourselves. This does not mean excusing our past behavior or ignoring our shortcomings. It means recognizing that we are inherently worthy of love and forgiveness because we are created in the image of the divine. When we let go of self-hate, we create space for self-compassion, allowing us to grow and change in meaningful ways.

This step challenges us to see ourselves and others through the eyes of divine innocence. It reminds us that even in our wolfish moments, we are not beyond redemption. By making a list of those we have harmed and becoming willing to make amends, we take an important step toward healing, both within ourselves and in our relationships. We acknowledge the power of love to overcome hate, and we move closer to the truth of who we are: beings of divine innocence, capable of creating peace, reconciliation, and harmony in the world around us.

Step 9: Responsibility
Make direct amends to such people wherever possible, except when doing so would injure them or others.

This step calls us to take responsibility for our actions by righting our wrongs. It is a pivotal part of the process of returning to divine innocence, as it involves actively repairing the damage caused by our wolfish behaviors. The act of making amends is not merely about saying "I'm sorry"; it is about demonstrating genuine remorse through action and seeking to restore relationships in a meaningful way.

Whenever possible, we should approach those we have harmed with humility and a sincere desire to make things right. This is an opportunity to show love, courage, and integrity. By facing the consequences of our actions, we honor the divine innocence within ourselves and the people we have wronged. Each attempt at reconciliation, no matter the outcome, is a step toward rebuilding the home of our soul and reinforcing the walls of our divine innocence.

However, it is essential to approach this step with discernment and prayer. While making amends is an important act of love, there are times when doing so directly may cause more harm than good. For example, if reaching out to someone would reopen old wounds, disrupt their healing process, or endanger their safety, it may not be appropriate to make direct contact. In such cases, we must find alternative ways to make amends that honor the principle of restoration without causing further injury.

Symbolic acts of amends can take many forms. They might involve making a donation to a charity that aligns with the values of the person we harmed, volunteering our time in a way that reflects our commitment to change, or writing a heartfelt letter that we do not send but use as a way to process and acknowledge our actions. These symbolic gestures allow us to take responsibility for our wrongs while respecting the well-being of others.

It is also important to remember that making amends does not guarantee forgiveness or reconciliation. The other person may not be ready or willing to accept our apology or to rebuild the relationship. While this can be painful, it does not diminish the value of taking responsibility. The act of making amends is ultimately about aligning ourselves with divine innocence and showing that we are committed to living in a way that reflects love, honesty, and accountability.

This step challenges us to let go of our pride and self-interest, to put others' well-being above our desire for absolution or closure. It calls us to act in love and humility, trusting that even if our efforts are not received as we hope, they are still meaningful and transformative. By taking responsibility for our actions, we begin to repair the damage caused by the wolf within us and pave the way for healing and renewal —not only for others but also for ourselves.

In essence, Step Nine is a practice of accountability, compassion, and discernment. It teaches us to balance our desire to make amends with the wisdom to recognize when and how to do so in a way that is truly restorative. By embracing this responsibility, we move closer to the divine innocence that is our true home, building stronger relationships and a stronger foundation for our lives.

Step 10: Discipline
Continue to take personal inventory, and when we are wrong, promptly admit it.

This step calls us to practice daily self-awareness and accountability, ensuring that we remain vigilant against the wolf within us. By regularly examining our thoughts, actions, and motives, we cultivate the discipline needed to recognize when we have veered from the path of divine innocence. When we acknowledge our mistakes and promptly admit them, we prevent the wolf from gaining a foothold in our lives and strengthen our connection to innocence.

Life is inherently filled with challenges, and we will inevitably face wolves huffing and puffing at our doors. Whether those wolves appear as external pressures, interpersonal conflicts, or internal temptations, our ability to remain in innocence depends on how we respond. Step Ten encourages us to reflect on our choices, learn from our experiences, and course-correct when necessary. This is not a one-time effort but an ongoing practice of humility, courage, and faith.

Maintaining innocence requires us to avoid the fight-or-flight response that characterizes the wolf. Instead, we must take a step back, assess the situation with a clear mind, and choose actions that align with the principles of love, truth, and divine guidance. When the wolf is at our door, we can resist the urge to react impulsively and instead respond with intentionality and wisdom.

Two practical steps can help us stay grounded in innocence when faced with challenges. The first is to seek wise counsel from like-minded, innocent friends or mentors. These individuals can offer perspective, encouragement, and guidance, helping us navigate difficult situations without succumbing to the wolf's tactics. Their support reminds us that we are not alone and that we can draw strength from our relationships with others.

The second step is to pray for divine guidance and clarity. By turning to God in moments of uncertainty or conflict, we open ourselves to the wisdom and peace that come from trusting His will. Prayer helps us remain centered, focused, and aligned with our true selves, even in the face of adversity.

Admitting when we are wrong is a powerful act of humility that keeps us rooted in innocence. It allows us to repair relationships, learn from our mistakes, and grow stronger in our faith and character. When we promptly acknowledge our missteps, we prevent guilt, shame, or pride from taking root and giving the wolf an opportunity to thrive within us.

Step Ten is ultimately about staying vigilant and proactive in our journey toward divine innocence. It requires discipline, honesty, and a willingness to face the truth about ourselves every day. By committing to this ongoing practice, we fortify the walls of our souls and create a life that reflects the strength, love, and integrity of our true nature. Through this discipline, we ensure that our homes remain places of peace and refuge, impervious to the wolf's huffing and puffing.

Step 11: Spiritual Awareness
Seek through prayer and meditation to improve our conscious contact with God, praying only for knowledge of His will for us and the power to carry that out.

Step Eleven is about deepening our connection to God and nurturing our divine innocence by becoming attuned to His presence and guidance. Through prayer and meditation, we open ourselves to a relationship with God that goes beyond words and rituals. It becomes a living, breathing awareness of His will in our lives and the strength to follow it.

In this step, the focus shifts from asking for specific outcomes to seeking alignment with God's will. This requires humility, trust, and patience. We pray not for what we think we need, but for clarity about what God desires for us and the courage to act on that understanding. This surrender is a powerful act of faith that leads to peace, guidance, and a deeper sense of purpose.

One of the most profound ways to engage with this step is through listening prayer. Unlike active prayers where we speak our thoughts or requests, listening prayer invites us to quiet our minds and hearts, creating space for God to speak. We ask for His thoughts and then wait, trusting that He will communicate with us in ways we can understand. These messages may come as impressions in our hearts, whispers in our minds, or signs in our daily lives.

Meditation complements prayer by helping us become more receptive to God's presence. It allows us to quiet the noise of the world and the distractions of our own minds, fostering an inner stillness where we can hear God's voice more clearly. A simple practice of focusing on our breath or repeating a short prayer or verse can bring us into a state of peace and openness.

Spending time in nature is another powerful way to connect with God and nurture spiritual awareness. In the beauty of creation, we can experience His presence in a tangible and inspiring way. The rustling of leaves, the flow of a stream, or the vastness of the sky reminds us of His majesty and our place within His design. Nature quiets the mind, softens the heart, and invites us to return to the innocence that is our divine inheritance.

As we deepen our spiritual awareness, we become more sensitive to the ways God is working in our lives. We notice His hand in the small details and the larger patterns of our experiences. We begin to trust that even the challenges we face are part of a greater plan for our growth and ultimate good. This awareness strengthens our faith and empowers us to live with integrity, courage, and love.

Step Eleven is a call to cultivate an ongoing dialogue with God, one that permeates every aspect of our lives. By seeking His will and relying on His power, we align ourselves with the divine flow of life. We become instruments of His love and wisdom, able to face the world with the strength and confidence that comes from walking in His light. This practice not only brings us closer to God but also helps us remain firmly rooted in our innocence, no matter what challenges or wolves we may encounter.

Step 12: Service

Having had a spiritual awakening as a result of these steps, carry this message to others and practice these principles in all our affairs

Step Twelve is the culmination of our journey, the point at which our transformation becomes not just an internal experience but an outward expression of our newfound innocence. It is here that we fully embrace the responsibility of living out the principles we have learned. Through our actions, interactions, and choices, we carry the message of divine innocence into the world, becoming beacons of light for others.

Service is not merely about helping others; it is about embodying a way of being that reflects our spiritual awakening. It is about approaching others with love, compassion, humility, and integrity. It means listening without judgment, offering support without expectation, and showing kindness even when it is not reciprocated. This is how we demonstrate the power of divine innocence to transform lives, including our own.

Carrying this message to others does not require grand gestures or public declarations. It can be as simple as sharing our story when someone is struggling or being a source of calm and reassurance in moments of chaos. Often, our actions speak louder than our words. When people see the peace, resilience, and authenticity that divine innocence has brought to our lives, they may be inspired to embark on their own journey of transformation.

Practicing these principles in all our affairs means that our commitment to innocence extends beyond our personal relationships. It touches every aspect of our lives, from how we approach our work to how we interact with strangers. It challenges us to maintain our integrity in difficult situations and to choose love over fear, even when it is hard.

In many ways, Step Twelve is a return to the first step but from a place of strength and awareness. We are now equipped to recognize the wolf within and around us, to resist its influence, and to live in alignment with our divine nature. By staying grounded in these principles, we build homes that are not only strong enough to withstand the wolf's attacks but also warm and welcoming to those who seek refuge and guidance.

This step is also a reminder that the journey is ongoing. Spiritual awakening is not a destination but a way of life. Each day presents new opportunities to learn, grow, and deepen our connection to God and to others. As we continue to practice these steps, we find that our capacity for love, understanding, and service expands. We become more attuned to the divine flow of life and more committed to sharing its blessings with the world.

In serving others, we strengthen our own innocence. By carrying this message and practicing these principles, we create ripples of positive change that extend far beyond ourselves. In this way, Step Twelve is both an ending and a beginning—a call to live fully in the light of divine innocence and to help others do the same.

Embracing Transformation

Renouncing the wolf and reclaiming our innocence is not a one-time event. It is a lifelong process that requires vigilance, humility, and faith. It requires us to look inward when faced with conflict, to recognize our own tendencies toward anger, manipulation, or fear, and to choose a different path.

The beauty of this journey is that each step we take toward divine innocence strengthens us. With every act of self-reflection, every prayer, and every effort to reconcile with those we have harmed, we build stronger walls around our homes. These walls are not barriers that isolate us from others but protective boundaries that keep the wolf at bay while allowing us to thrive in harmony with those who share our values.

Ultimately, embracing divine innocence is about living in alignment with our true selves, rooted in love, compassion, and humility. It is about recognizing that we are not perfect, but we are perfectly loved. When we trust in that love, we find the strength to withstand any attack, to rebuild when necessary, and to shine as beacons of light in a world that often feels dark. The wolf may still howl at our doors, but we can rest easy, knowing that our homes— built on the solid foundation of divine innocence—will stand firm.

One of our ways of serving others in divine innocence is to write.

We feel compelled by our individual innocence to share in all authenticity and honesty what God has placed in our hearts and in our lives. Specifically, for me (Robert), this means bringing light to the darkness of autism so that others might come to understand the autistic mind and benefit from its gifts.

Final Thoughts About the Wolf

Life will always include a certain amount of chaos, and our task is to build a house strong enough to withstand the storms without shutting ourselves off from the world. This strength, grounded in divine innocence, allows us to navigate life's challenges while remaining true to who we are.

The connection between people and wolves is undeniable, as every person harbors a wolf nature within them. However, the difference lies in how we respond to that nature. We must consciously decide not to act as the wolf in moments of challenge or threat. When we fail to make this choice, the wolf takes over, driving our actions, words, and thoughts from a place of ignorance rather than innocence. The wolf thrives in the natural world of competition and domination, seeking to suppress the divine innocence that is our true inheritance.

On the surface, the wolf can appear enticing. It may seem powerful, organized, and even good. Wolves hunt, live, and play together as a pack, unified in their goals and protective of one another. But this unity comes at a cost. Within the pack, there is no freedom for the individual; conformity is demanded, and deviation leads to instant and irreversible ostracism. The wolf seems to embody courage, strength, loyalty, and wisdom, but these qualities are only skin deep. Beneath the surface, the wolf's actions are driven by a constant

"The wolf's actions are driven by a constant need to maintain a competitive edge."

need to maintain a competitive edge, one that is perpetually challenged and can be lost at any moment.

In truth, the wolf knows nothing of divine innocence. Its entire existence is based on lies—deceptions designed to consolidate power and control. Wolves use lies to dominate others, building entire worlds of falsehoods that center on their supposed superiority. These lies are often effective because they prey on our innocent nature. As humans, we are wired to trust. We yearn for validation and connection rooted in truth, trust, and faith, and this makes us susceptible to the wolf's manipulations. Wolves exploit this trust through glitz, glamour, empty promises, and carefully crafted illusions of dominance.

At the core of the wolf's behavior is a deep sense of inadequacy and inferiority. The wolf's desperate attempts to gain power and control over others are a way to compensate for these feelings. Whether through direct means like intimidation or indirect means like manipulation and deceit, the wolf seeks to mask its inner vulnerabilities. But no amount of control can fill the void left by the wolf's abandonment of innocence.

What separates humans from wolves is not our physical traits like opposable thumbs or the ability to speak. It is our capacity for divine innocence. Humans have the ability to dream, learn, empathize, forgive, and envision the future. These gifts have the potential to elevate the human soul and bring harmony to the world. But when we abandon these gifts, choosing instead the path of the wolf, we become destructive not just to nature but to one another. The further we stray from innocence, the more we devalue life itself.

To deny our ability to dream or to accept someone else's dream as our own is to surrender to the wolf. This often begins in childhood, when parents or authority figures impose their dreams onto us. My own mother repeatedly told my brothers and me never to get married or have children, warning that if we did, she would disown us (Robert). Her demand was born from a fear of losing her place in our hearts and minds. My brothers conformed to her wishes, sacrificing their own dreams to gain her approval. I, however, realized at the age of ten that her love was conditional, that I would never truly have her approval. It was a painful truth, but it freed me. In that moment, I let go of her dreams for me and embraced my own.

Recognizing and pursuing our own dreams is critical to living in divine innocence. A dream imposed by someone else is always a lie. Our true dream can only come from within, revealed by the still, quiet voice of our divine innocence.

When we choose the wolf, we betray that innocence. We fight

against our own divine nature and the life we were meant to live. But when we recognize the wolf within and make the conscious choice to return to innocence, we reclaim the power and freedom that are our birthright.

WOLF QUIZ

Within each chapter, you might recall that there are wolf questions associated with each builder type. Those questions reflect the more general characteristics of the wolf that you have learned in this chapter. Take some time to honestly reflect on each of the following questions to determine the extent to which you exhibit wolfish behaviors.

Answer each question using the following scale:

1 Never

2 Rarely

3 Sometimes

4 Often

5 Always

1. I interrogate, punish, or indict others without feeling guilty, before investigating all the facts.

    1 - 2 - 3 - 4 - 5

2. I conspire to destroy other people's life's work, dreams, or aspirations regardless of the outcome or fallout, and I feel no remorse.

    1 - 2 - 3 - 4 - 5

3. I disregard the sanctity of other people's beliefs or spiritual faith because I know the truth.

    1 - 2 - 3 - 4 - 5

4. I seek to harm myself and/or others around me regardless of the consequences.

    1 - 2 - 3 - 4 - 5

5. I use anger as a method of controlling others.

    1 - 2 - 3 - 4 - 5

6. I name-call, belittle, or speak badly about others behind their backs when I believe they deserve it.

    1 - 2 - 3 - 4 - 5

7. I hide, withhold, or skew information that would reveal someone's innocence or my own guilt.

    1 - 2 - 3 - 4 - 5

8. I avoid admitting I am wrong, even when I know I am. 1 - 2 - 3 - 4 - 5

9. Deep down, I believe that meekness is weakness.

    1 - 2 - 3 - 4 - 5

10. I support violent behavior if it serves a purpose I believe in.

    1 - 2 - 3 - 4 - 5

11. I am quick to anger, even when I know I shouldn't be. 1 - 2 - 3 - 4 - 5

12. I skew the truth to protect myself.

    1 - 2 - 3 - 4 - 5

13. I lack self-control.

    1 - 2 - 3 - 4 - 5

14. I think I'm worthless.

   1 - 2 - 3 - 4 - 5

15. I feel like my life is difficult because other people don't treat me right.

   1 - 2 - 3 - 4 - 5

How to Score the Quiz:

The Wolf: A score between 60-75 indicates more wolf-like tendencies and ignorance of your actions. You are most certainly living as the wolf if you scored in this range.

The Pig: A score between 30-59 indicates that you are living in divine innocence most of the time. Your lower score shows that you have greater awareness and commitment to living in innocence. You are aware of your behavior and are striving toward divine innocence. Like the rest of us, you do not always succeed but you recognize when you are being the wolf.

The Wolf in Disguise: A score between 15-29 likely indicates that you are in denial about your wolfish tendencies and are likely acting as the wolf in ways that you are unaware of. You are the wolf in disguise, as the wolf who dressed as grandma in Little Red Riding Hood. The "never" response is most significant—if you consistently claim to never engage in wolfish behavior, it may indicate denial or an inability to recognize your own actions.

If you scored above 60 or under 30 on this quiz, take some time to self-reflect and seek your holy innocence through prayer and study. In this way, you can find your way back to your divine innocence and live joyfully and peacefully as your true builder type. If you know your builder type, return to that chapter and implement the techniques we have shown you here to return to innocence.

CHAPTER 7

INHABITANTS OF THE CYCLE

We are all inhabitants of the wolf cycle. We each have a choice of whether to participate in the cycle as pigs or wolves, as innocents or ignoramuses. It is a moment by moment, day by day choice. Sometimes we will encounter the wolf in someone and that will trigger our wolf to snarl and rear its ugly head. Sometimes we find out, suddenly, that we have been living our whole lives as the wolf. By definition, the wolf does not recognize itself as the wolf. This is why we have used the term ignorance to describe the wolf in this book. Wolves, as you recall, are ignorant of their innocence. In this chapter, my goal is to show you examples of people you know (and people I (Robert) know) who have chosen to live as pigs or wolves so that you might recognize them in your own life.

Before we explore these examples, it is important to recognize how pigs and wolves interact with each other in a general sense. What comes to my mind is the proverb 'birds of a feather flock together.' This adage became a part of our common wisdom for a reason it is true. If we stop and ponder, or even bluntly ask ourselves, 'why are we friends with our closest friends?' then we will likely begin with a list of the things we like about them. Sure, there is the commonality of growing up in the same community or belonging to the same religion, enjoying the same type of foods, activities, maybe even the same economic class and so on. But there may be something else, something that is grounded in whether we choose to live in our innocence or our ignorance (in our pig nature or our wolf).

That 'something else' connects us together outside of our commonalities. Pigs who have not been traumatized will be naturally wary of a wolf that attempts to infiltrate their lives. They will be uncomfortable with a wolf who tries to befriend them. These pigs will connect only with other pigs. So what happens when a pig is traumatized or even raised by wolves? They will, tragically, seek the company of wolves, thus driving them toward destruction.

Wolves, on the other hand, tend to hang out with other wolves… with one exception. Wolves will seek out pigs to use for their gain. Wolves seek to consume the pigs–whether that be through using the pigs' talents, emotional energy, skills, or dreams. Even though wolves may seem to accept pigs into their inner circles, they do not recognize the pigs as truly part of the group. They only recognize other wolves as such. The pigs they invite in are there purely for the pigs' own demise, because the wolves are so sure that they can dominate them.

To see this dynamic between wolves and pigs more clearly, think of the inventor whose business partner files for the patent under his own name and squeezes out the inventor. This is a wolf consuming a pig. Think of the child who is bullied by others on the playground because they have a gentle nature. This is a wolf attacking a pig. Think of the person on a first date who hears their date speak harshly of their past loves and decides not to pursue a second date. This is a pig rejecting a wolf.

In the following stories, you will find examples of wolves and pigs intermingling with one another. These stories are from my personal life as well as famous examples in history. It is helpful to you at this point in the book, dear reader, because it will strengthen your ability to recognize wolves and pigs in your environment. It will also enable you to identify the personalities of people you encounter. Recognizing whether someone is a natural straw, stick or brick helps you decide how you want to move the conversation or relationship forward or whether you want to avoid this new person altogether. You will learn to notice when a wolf is attempting to manipulate you, and you will know to move away from them. You may also just decide to have fun interacting with them, and knowing their nature enables you to communicate effectively and enjoy your interactions. Of course, at all times, you must realize your boundaries so that you do not become the wolf yourself. Additionally, you will want to remember that people are emotional subjects so it's important not to manipulate them on the basis of the techniques and ideas in this book. Manipulation is always an act of the wolf.

You might ask, is it possible to disarm the wolf? The answer is no. Those who play with fire will get burned. You cannot disarm him, but you can disempower him because his only power is found in consuming you. When you don't play his games, he goes away dejected and powerless. The way to defeat the evil of the wolf is to never give him an opportunity to consume you, and you do this through maintaining your innocence, your strength, and never give him anything. This is how Jesus did it.

Remember, his only strength is found in consuming your strength. Wolves are inherently ignorant, because they are ignoring their only source of power (i.e. their innocence). They seek power and strength by consuming the innocence of others, all in an effort to fill the emptiness within them where their innocence lies. Yet it is not that they do not have innocence–they do. But they are ignorant of it. That, my friend, is why the wolves are ignorant.

You cannot solve their problem of ignorance. You cannot bring them back to innocence. They must do this for themselves. Just as an addict must decide for themselves that they are ready to stop using because they can only get sober for themselves, the wolf must decide that they want to be innocent.

When an innocent pig attempts to join a wolf pack, which they might do because of the charisma of wolves and the allure of their world, first of all that pig is fooling himself. Nothing good can come of it for the pig. The wolves will consume him. Unless, that is, he succumbs to his own wolf nature and fully immerses himself in the culture of the wolves. If he remains an innocent pig, he will be consumed, used by the wolves until he is no longer of use to them and then discarded like so much trash.

Bernie Madoff and the Wolves of Wall Street

Bernie Madoff is an example of how wolves act with one another and how their friend groups work. It is also an instance of how innocent pigs can be bamboozled and their fortunes (their financial homes) destroyed by wolves in their midst. Court records indicate he began a Ponzi scheme against investors starting in the early 1960s. He ran it successfully for decades because of a dedicated team of people willing to falsify trade reports for him and because he was always able to keep up with investors' demands for dividends by bringing in new investors. All of the people in his inner circle who helped him were wolves in his pack.

By the 1990s, there were a few business people in the financial industry that knew his operations were not legitimate, and one of them, Harry Markopolos, reported him to the SEC in 1999. The SEC did not do their due diligence against Madoff at that time, and as a result he was able to snooker trusting investors for another nine years,[1] all because the officials were lazy and not willing to pursue the warning

---

[1] https://www.forbes.com/sites/richardbehar/2024/07/31/how-many-red-flags-did-my-aunt-adele-need-on-her-madoff-statements/

signs. The checks and balances of the industry failed, because of the wolfishness of these officials and those willing to help–or ignore– Madoff. After Madoff's empire fell in 2008, the life savings of many innocent people were wiped out, including charities. In its wake, people committed suicide, including Madoff's own son.

Wolves compete by attempting to beat out other wolves in whatever game they play. To feed themselves, wolves hunt in packs. This is how they interact with those outside of their in-group. Jordan Belfort, about whom the film *The Wolf of Wall Street* was made, is another great example. At one time, he employed 1000 stock brokers who sold penny stocks in what the financial industry calls pump-and-dump stocks, ultimately defrauding investors of more than $200 million. The title itself speaks to the premise of this book. Inside their group, they have a hierarchy that is hard-fought and won by the dominant wolves. The submissive wolves accept their place, unless they see an opportunity to fight and win against a wolf higher in the pack than themselves. If they see such a place, they will quickly and with a sense of moral rightness begin the fight. If they win, they assume their new place in the hierarchy. If they lose, they are killed, forced out of the pack, and then demonized and exiled. If they survive, they must set out on their own in search of a new pack. We see evidence of this dynamic in our society. Phrases such as 'rat race,' 'keeping up with the Joneses,' and 'living on a hamster wheel' all speak to the culture of wolves.

Tom and the Innocence of Connection

For our second example of an inhabitant of the *Wolf Cycle*, let's consider my recent acquaintance, Tom. I met him at a local event—a folk dance hosted by a contra club. I arrived on time at 7 PM, only to find the hall nearly empty. There were just two people present: Tom and me. The band was at the back of the hall, tuning their instruments, but other than that, no one else was there—not even the hosts of the dance. I was surprised. Later, I learned that 7–8 PM was just a practice time and the actual dance started at 8.

At that moment, without knowing this, it occurred to me that the way we perceive and respond to time reveals a truth about ourselves. Timeliness, as a habit, is often driven by one of three motivations, which can provide insights into whether someone is a stick, straw, or brick builder—or even a wolf. A straw builder values timeliness because they see time itself as a precious resource to be measured and utilized. A stick builder values punctuality because they value their word and the commitment they've made. A brick builder shows up on time out of respect for the event and their role in it. In contrast, wolves only respect punctuality when it serves their interests. While showing up on time doesn't tell the whole story, it's one piece of the puzzle that hints at a person's builder type.

Seeing only Tom and myself in the hall, I faced a common dilemma: Should I acknowledge his presence, or should I keep to myself since we were strangers? This reminded me of how often people pass one another on the street without a word, ignoring the humanity in those around them. To me, this feels like a blatant disregard for another person's value. I chose to introduce myself. Walking over, I extended my hand and said, "Hi, I'm Robert."

Tom replied, "I'm Tom."

I've trained myself to identify people I meet as sticks, straws, or bricks. To strike up a conversation, I began with a simple yet revealing question: "What work do you do?" A person's past or current occupation often offers clues about their builder type.

Tom answered, "I'm a retired mechanical engineer."

Based on his profession, I made an initial guess that Tom was a straw personality. Straws often enjoy discussions about facts, data, science, and measurable outcomes, as well as being voracious readers. Since I'm a stick, conversations with a straw can sometimes require precision in language, but I decided to start with something I thought would impress him: my upcoming book. Telling him I was about to publish a memoir seemed more fitting than mentioning my work as a horse boarder. Writing a book is generally impressive to a stick but even more so to a straw. If Tom had been a stick or a brick, I might have led with my horse boarding business and mentioned my writing later.

Straws also tend to value connections that they can use to bolster their credibility. If you give them a reason to name-drop you as a reputable connection, they'll often value the interaction even more.

After I told Tom about my book, he asked what it was about. I explained that my first book was a memoir, and my second was a personality book inspired by the story of *The Three Little Pigs*. Then I asked him, "Which house would you build?" I added, "Keep in mind, the pigs built their houses based on how their brains were wired, not just the materials available."

Tom paused, then said, "The straw house."

"I agree," I said with a smile.

"What does that mean?" he asked.

I explained, "It means you value facts, data, science, and measurable information from credible sources." Tom nodded in agreement. Then I added, "You're also very impatient."

This comment triggered a reaction. "Who told you I was impatient?" Tom asked, visibly annoyed.

"You did," I replied. "By virtue of being a straw builder. The pig who built the straw house built it quickly because he didn't want to spend a lot of time constructing his home. He'd rather spend his time doing more important things, like learning."

From our conversation, I could tell Tom wasn't a lazy straw. He spent his time wisely, studying, learning, and mastering his craft. Lazy straw builders, on the other hand, don't measure accurately or put in the effort, and their houses often fall apart. These types tend to present as know-it-alls, and I don't waste time engaging with them. But Tom and I gained mutual respect. As the band began to play, I wasn't sure if

Tom was as surprised by our interaction as I was, but I knew we had connected on a meaningful level.

Leigh and My Wolf of Complaining

Leigh and I met in 1988 at an Amway meeting. We were in our middle to late twenties, just a few years apart. Before diving into my story with Leigh, I need to touch on Amway itself. Many dismiss Amway as a "get rich quick scheme" because it operates as a multi-level marketing (MLM) company. They assume it is designed to make others rich at their expense. Nothing could be further from the truth.

If Amway were such a scheme, it would be a wolfish business. However, in my opinion, Amway never promises wealth without effort. On the contrary, it emphasizes the importance of upstanding character and sound business practices. They dedicate significant time to teaching these principles. Through Amway, I gained invaluable knowledge about financial literacy, interpersonal relationships, and failure. I also forged lifelong friendships. Most importantly, Amway introduced me to Jesus Christ.

From Amway, I learned good character and business practices— principles I was never taught in school. I credit these lessons for helping me achieve millionaire status. However, if you ignore these principles or lack strong character, you are more likely to go broke despite your efforts, because your focus is misaligned. This is why many people fail in Amway—they join for the money alone.

I admit, money was the hook that drew me into Amway, as it is for most people. But I came to realize that discipline and a purpose higher than financial gain are essential to success. Building an Amway business is much like earning a degree from an accredited college: there's no guarantee of financial independence, but it provides the foundation for potential success. Both require hard work, focus, and dedication. That is why most people fail in Amway, and why I ultimately failed as well.

My failure came down to one simple issue: I was a complainer. At first, my complaining was internal—an undercurrent of frustration and feeling put upon because success wasn't coming as quickly as I had hoped. I spent ten years trying to build my business without meaningful results. All the while, my inner negativity undermined my efforts.

It sounds strange now, but at the time, I did not realize I was being negative. For someone who prided himself on turning life's big negatives into positives, I had overlooked the importance of applying this mindset to smaller, everyday frustrations. In the end, my constant internal complaints spilled over into my outward interactions, and my prospects and affiliates sensed it.

Leigh was the one who finally held up the mirror and showed me the truth: complaining is the behavior of a wolf. When we're grounded in our divine innocence, we don't complain. Complaining is rooted in anger and resentment, and it corrodes relationships and opportunities.

Leigh and his wife had joined Amway through one of my prospects, and even after those prospects quit, Leigh and I remained committed. He later told me that I inspired him with my positivity, enthusiasm, and potential. He believed I was going somewhere in life, and I admired him for his drive to create a better future.

At the time, my inner negativity had not surfaced in a way others could see. I worked hard, eager to prove myself—to me, my spouse, and perhaps the world. I spent countless hours studying people's behavior, learning to approach new prospects, and overcoming my natural tendency to hide behind trees, cars, or bushes to avoid conversation. I even attracted a diverse range of people, from millionaires to those struggling to make ends meet. But I didn't know how to nurture or retain them, and most eventually left.

After ten years, my frustration grew, and my internal complaints became external. I voiced my discontent about how little long-term success I was achieving despite my efforts. Prospects left my circle as quickly as they entered, and my complaining only hastened their departures. Finally, I quit Amway, choosing instead to focus on raising my family. Leigh eventually left as well, finding that Amway was not moving fast enough for him either.

Years later, Leigh and I reconnected at my son's wedding. By then, he had gone through a divorce, and my wife was telling guests she planned to divorce me. A concerned guest informed me of her comments, making an already emotional day even more stressful.

Leigh seemed to sense my distress and made a special effort to reconnect with me. That day marked the renewal of our friendship.

Leigh became a source of unwavering support during one of the most challenging periods of my life. He believed in me, not because of my business success—or lack thereof—but because of who I was as a person. When I battled depression and suicidal thoughts, Leigh checked in on me, offering encouragement and helping me find my center. I did the same for him.

When I began writing and creating videos about my past, Leigh encouraged me to focus on the positives in my life alongside the hardships I had endured. It was Leigh who helped me see that my inner habit of complaining had been a major obstacle. His insight was a revelation, as I had always prided myself on turning life's negatives into positives.

Looking back, it is clear that my complaining undermined my efforts in Amway. My affiliates likely sensed my hesitation and corrosive attitude, even when I wasn't aware of it myself. Now, I am dedicated to battling this wolf-like tendency and embracing positivity in both my inner dialogue and outward actions. This shift has transformed my life, allowing me to achieve success in my horse business and writing like never before.

Complaining is truly a wolf's behavior—passive-aggressive and rooted in anger and resentment. It has no place in a life committed to innocence. By recognizing and rejecting this destructive tendency, we can build lives grounded in authenticity, gratitude, and positivity.

Dorothy and the Wolf of Illness

This is the story of my friend Dorothy and her battle with chronic sickness.

Before diving into Dorothy's story, I want to share something personal. When I was newly baptized into the Church of Jesus Christ of Latter-Day Saints at 22, I never felt that my same-sex attraction or my desire to be a mom was something I should feel guilty about. These feelings were mine and mine alone. They didn't define my worthiness to be baptized, and I never acted on them. To me, they weren't sinful; they were sacred. Innocence resides in truth, and in my mind, thoughts and feelings are truthful when they arise naturally, without action or intention to harm. This will become relevant as I tell Dorothy's story.

My friendship with Dorothy began after church one day. She approached me in the chapel lobby and said, "Hi, my name is Dorothy. I'm sick." Her unusual introduction startled me. Was she contagious? Should I step back? But I stayed where I was and replied, "Robert Bautner." She dabbed her nose with a tissue and quickly clarified, "I'm sick, but I don't have a cold or anything." Despite her words, Dorothy looked well: clear complexion, pleasant voice, and close to my age and height. She wasn't someone I felt attracted to, but I was comfortable speaking with her.

As we talked, she mentioned knowing my brother, Hermann, through her sister who had once dated him. This surprised me, as none of my brothers were the type to step into a church or maintain relationships for long. Dorothy changed the subject, mentioning her plans to attend college on a voice scholarship to study nutrition and modeling. Her calm demeanor and sweet voice intrigued me, but I struggled to connect her words to her self-proclaimed sickness. Why would someone introduce themselves that way?

Dorothy's words stayed with me. I later shared the encounter with friends who had known her since childhood, and they cautioned me: "She's always sick." Their reaction caught me off guard, but it explained her focus on illness. As the years went on, I watched Dorothy's health deteriorate. She went from walking on her own to using a cane to being wheelchair bound. Despite this, Dorothy remained cheerful and proved to be both artistic and accomplished. She composed poems, sang, and even won the Miss Wheelchair pageant. Her wheelchair did not limit her spirit, yet she persisted in her continual statements of sickness.

One day I realized how much her words had impacted me when my five-year-old son stood on our front steps and exclaimed, "Everything bad always happens to me!" His statement echoed Dorothy's refrain, "I'm sick." I couldn't let those words take root in his mind. I confronted him immediately and firmly told him never to say such things again. This pivotal moment, shaped by my experiences with Dorothy, taught me how powerful our words and beliefs are in shaping our lives.

Over time, I began to wonder if Dorothy's repeated declarations of illness were a shield. Did she use sickness to protect herself from something deeper? I hesitated to ask her, but the question nagged at me: "Did you will yourself into this wheelchair?" When I finally gathered the courage to ask, her response—a mix of tension and disbelief—prompted me to shift the conversation to my own experiences. I shared how, as a child, I had unconsciously blurred my vision to avoid seeing the chaos around me.

Dorothy later confided in me about her traumatic past, including instances of childhood and teenage rape. These experiences had profoundly affected her, and I came to understand that her creative pursuits—poetry, music, and art—were ways of balancing the deep pain she carried. Through her art, she expressed the beauty within her, even as her body bore the weight of her trauma. While I wouldn't recommend soothing the trauma of one's past with negative thoughts of illness, it did protect the light of divine innocence in her soul.

Our friendship continues to this day, and Dorothy remains a source of inspiration. She taught me the power of words and the importance of being mindful of the narratives we create for ourselves. Dorothy's story, with its mix of resilience and pain, showed me how the mind can transform adversity into creativity and how innocence can coexist with profound suffering.

Anastacio and the Innocence of Persistence

I have learned that labeling people who treat us poorly as 'toxic' can sometimes devolve into our own wolfish behavior. When we dismiss people or wish they did not exist because they appear to be wolves, we might inadvertently become the wolves ourselves. While there are times when we must distance ourselves from true wolves in our lives —even family members—there are also times when these labels and hard boundaries are harmful in and of themselves. Put another way, our interpretation of others' 'toxicity' often reflects the wolves in us. By avoiding so-called toxic people, we may miss hidden opportunities and unrealized adventures.

Some of the so-called 'toxic' people in my life have been pivotal in shaping who I am today. The key was remaining grounded in my innocence and not allowing the wolf in them to bring out the wolf in me. Instead, I stayed true to my nature as a stick builder. For this, I say thank you to all the wolves and so-called toxic people who knocked at my door. I'm grateful that my innocence interrupted their plot and that I did not react to their intrusions.

This brings me to Anastacio and his story. I met Anastacio while working with my son Parker on a client's lawn. I saw him approaching and instinctively stopped my equipment to ensure his safety. He stopped too, taking it as an invitation to talk.

"Hello señor, do you have any work for me?" he asked.

Caught off guard, I replied, "I don't speak Spanish."

"But I'm speaking to you in English," he said, smiling.

I quickly deflected, pointing him toward Parker, who had recently returned from a church mission and spoke fluent Spanish. I knew Parker would not hire him—we did not hire employees. Ours was a simple business without payroll complications. Anastacio walked over to Parker, and they talked for several minutes.

After Anastacio left, Parker told me he had given Anastacio his number and suggested he call his mother, who ran a garden center. He then explained that Anastacio had quit his job earlier that day because his manager was verbally abusive. To add insult to injury, he was then denied transportation by the bus driver because his transfer had expired two minutes earlier. As a result, he was walking home when he encountered us—a journey of ten miles. I would never have known he had had such a difficult morning. He had been cheerful and optimistic when he approached.

A few days later, Anastacio's wife Laura called Parker and thanked him, telling him she had turned in Anastacio's application. She explained that she was undergoing chemotherapy and could not work, leaving Anastacio as their sole provider. He was hired immediately and began working long, hard hours. Laura also texted me to thank me for helping her husband, though I felt I had done little beyond directing him to Parker. I couldn't shake the guilt of my initial reaction: "I don't speak Spanish."

Laura and Anastacio's story didn't stop at him being hired at the garden center. While Anastacio worked tirelessly to support his family, his commitment to learning and improving was unshakable. He paid close attention to every detail of the landscaping business, from planting trees and flowers to understanding the financial side of things. Though his English was limited, he took every challenge in stride, demonstrating a quiet determination that I came to admire deeply.

Three years into his job, Anastacio decided to ask for a raise. Despite being the hardest and most reliable worker, his request was met with dismissal. My wife told him, "You don't have a license, and you can't drive," implying that his limitations outweighed his contributions. Rather than becoming angry or bitter, Anastacio chose to walk away. With gratitude and grace, he handed back his tool belt and said, "Thank you so much for everything you've taught me. I quit."

That moment was a turning point for Anastacio. Instead of viewing his departure as a loss, he saw it as an opportunity. Drawing on the skills and knowledge he had gained, he decided to start his own landscaping business. With Laura's support, Anastacio poured his energy into building a business that reflected his values: hard work, integrity, and service. He applied everything he had learned, not just about landscaping, but about treating others with kindness—even those who had treated him poorly.

When I called Anastacio and Laura to gather details for this chapter, Laura shared how much their family's trajectory had changed. She told me, "You and Parker were the turning point for our family's future. That moment on the sidewalk set us on a path we never expected." I could see why she would say this. Their children had even started their own landscaping businesses, inspired by their father's example. Laura added, "Anastacio teaches his employees that if they want a job, they'll always find one. But if they want to build a successful business, they must always please the customer."

Anastacio's story is a testament to the power of divine innocence. Despite facing wolves in many forms—unreasonable managers, a dismissive bus driver, and even my initial hesitation—he never allowed bitterness or resentment to take root. Instead, he met every challenge with grace and determination, learning what he could and moving forward. His example reminds me that even when others appear toxic, they can still play a role in our growth if we respond from a place of innocence.

As I reflected on Anastacio's journey, I realized that the small, seemingly inconsequential moments—like a chance meeting on a sidewalk—can have generational impacts. Laura's message, 'You've impacted not just us but our children too,' humbled me. It was a reminder that by remaining true to our divine innocence and refraining from labeling others as wolves too quickly, we can create ripples of goodness that extend far beyond ourselves.

We ended our call with a promise to meet for dinner soon. I couldn't help but smile, knowing that Anastacio and Laura's story wasn't just a chapter in my book—it was a testament to resilience, kindness, and the transformative power of meeting life's challenges with the grace of divine innocence.

Jay and the Wolf of Sour Grapes

One day, during a phone call, Jay exclaimed, "I am so bummed!"

I asked, "What are you so bummed about?"

Jay said, "The man who was selling me monarch butterflies in California went out of business."

I asked, "He went bankrupt?"

"No, he had his business up for sale, and nobody bought it. Since no one bought it, he sold off the greenhouses and land and retired. I didn't even know his business was up for sale. Apparently, it had been on the market for quite some time. I don't understand why he didn't tell his customers. Now it's all gone—his greenhouses, his land, everything. That man sold over 50,000 butterflies a year. I was buying thousands of them from him at $4 each wholesale and selling them to my customers for $12 to $15 apiece."

I quickly calculated the numbers—hundreds of butterflies per event added up to thousands of dollars in business. "That's too bad," I said. I had known for a while that one of Jay's side gigs involved butterfly exhibits for municipalities and businesses. These events included up-close interactions with monarch butterflies, educational talks about their endangered status, and the grand finale: releasing hundreds of them into the wild. I had attended one of his events and was amazed by the turnout and enthusiasm from both children and adults. It was clear that losing this butterfly supplier was a significant blow to Jay's income and the communities he served.

Jay lamented, "I would have sold my home and moved to California if I'd known. I don't know what I'm going to do now."

The monarch butterfly industry, as Jay later explained, is tightly regulated by the USDA. Butterflies raised west of the Rocky Mountains cannot be sold east of the Continental Divide and vice versa. This is based on the belief that the populations are two distinct species, though breeders argue otherwise. Jay shared these details during his shows, explaining how habitat loss—particularly the eradication of milkweed—was driving monarchs toward extinction.

Hearing Jay's frustration, I said, "Since I own a farm, why don't we go into the butterfly business and raise them like the man in California did?"

Jay replied, "Nah, it's too much work. Monarchs are fragile. They can get a parasite called OE (Ophryocystis Elektroscirrha) from the milkweed they eat. It weakens them, causes deformities, and often leads to an early death."

His reservations did not make sense to me, given that he had said he would have moved to California had he known. I shrugged it off. It still sounded like a good business idea to me. Soon afterward, I was speaking with my son Parker and I brought up the subject. "You should look into the butterfly business," I suggested. "If you work it right, it could be a half-million to a million-dollar venture."

Parker did not respond immediately, later telling me he felt he did not have the time to raise butterflies. But a few weeks later, Jay encouraged Parker, saying, "If you start raising butterflies, I'll buy them from you." Still, Parker hesitated. But the tipping point came when an aquatic paradise company asked him to supply butterflies for a new exhibit. Within six weeks, Parker purchased a microscope and started studying butterfly care. With his first order, Parker netted $500.

At that time, the industry was primarily run by older people on the brink of retirement. As a collective body, they were concerned about the future of the butterflies without people like them raising them. When they got word of Parker, a young man, starting a butterfly business, they took notice. Within a few months, the International Butterflies and Breeders Association (IBBA) invited him to join its Board of Directors.

I was proud of Parker. What I did not know was that my friendship with Jay was about to end because of Parker's success. Jay and I had spoken two to three times a day everyday. We would talk about anything, from politics and world events to life and family. One day the phone stopped ringing.

Within a few weeks of Parker being put on the IBBA's board, Jay made one last phone call to meet. We met for a few minutes. Jay was infuriated. He wanted to know, "How did we go from talking about a man selling his butterfly business to Parker being on the IBBA's board of directors in a few months' time?"

I said, "I offered to go into the butterfly business with you, and you turned me down. So I told Parker about it and encouraged him."

"You never asked me to go into the business with you."

I repeated that I had indeed talked to him about it.

He replied, "You should have insisted that I do it."

I was flabbergasted. He was a 54-year-old man. Why would I twist his arm, disrespecting him by insisting that he follow up on the idea? He was rationalizing his sour grapes.

There was no reasoning with him. Jay disowned me, claiming I stole his idea. It was stranger still because he himself had encouraged Parker by telling Parker that he would buy butterflies from him if Parker raised them.

Sour grapes. He was so jealous of Parker's overnight success that he harbored resentment in his heart that turned to bitterness. That bitterness was primarily directed at me, but it did extend to Parker and eventually to my younger son Michael when he joined Parker as a business partner.

There was no going back. Jay began badmouthing me to everyone we knew in common. He told my relatives and our common friends, "Robert stole my idea. I'll never tell anybody anything ever again."

Nothing could be further from the truth, and it hurts to be misrepresented. More than that, it hurt to lose my good friend.

Jay kept his promise. He never spoke with me again. His bitterness extended so far that one day when I went to Subway and he was there, he looked me square in the eye, picked up his food, and left without a word.

This experience highlighted to me how differently people can perceive the same conversation and how even the smallest decisions can reflect either our innocence or our ignorance. Those perceptions can begin or end a relationship without us even knowing it. Jay's wolf of sour grapes consumed him, but Parker and I stayed grounded in our innocence, which allowed us to move forward in positivity and purpose.

Parker, Michael and I: The Innocence of Partnership

My son Parker has always been a hard worker who maintains his innocence in everything he does. When he saw the potential in the butterfly business, he decided to pursue it, transitioning from the plant business to butterflies. Despite the challenges of balancing his new venture with his responsibilities to his family of three children, Parker persisted. In 2019, he grossed about $32,000 from his butterfly business.

When the pandemic hit in early 2020, doubts briefly clouded his progress. Out of concern, Parker placed an ad for butterfly kits on Facebook one Thursday morning. By Saturday, the ad had gone viral, and he had received 500 orders. To meet the overwhelming demand, Parker called in every available family member to help process orders and respond to emails. With the support of his wife, sisters, and others, Parker delivered on his promises, and River Bottom Butterflies was born.

Still, Parker was running the business on the side with most of his attention remaining on his plant business. I watched him struggle to manage the operational details, recognizing the imbalance in his approach. As a brick builder, Parker was diligent and reliable, but I believed his business would benefit from the contributions of a straw and stick personality. This is where his younger brother Michael came into the picture.

Michael, a straw builder, had recently been laid off from his corporate job at a major food distributor. His passion for the environment made Parker's butterfly business especially intriguing to him. Before long, Michael joined Parker, and their wives also became involved. Together, they decided that their measurable goal was to repopulate the monarch butterfly and other species like red admirals, painted ladies, yellow sulfurs, and cabbage whites. Together, they propelled the business forward, grossing $98,000 in 2020, $195,000 in

2021, $250,000 in 2022, and nearing $375,000 by the end of 2023, and $450,000 at the time of this writing. When I originally told Parker he had a half-million to a million-dollar business on his hands, I had underestimated its potential. As a proud father, I can confidently say Parker and Michael have earned many "attaboys" from me.

While Parker and Michael thrived together, I initially thought their business was missing a third leg—a stick personality to balance the operation, like a sturdy three-legged stool on uneven terrain. At the time, I did not consider myself as that third leg, but in truth, I was a silent partner all along. Owning the farm that provided the foundation for their business and encouraging Parker from the start were my contributions to their success.

What began as a casual conversation grew into what will someday be a multi-million-dollar enterprise. The continued success of their business—and any business—rests on a strong foundation built by straw, stick, and brick-minded people working together. Excluding the wolf, I believe their success will only continue to grow.

Final Thoughts

After reading these stories, I am imagining that you also have people and situations coming to mind. Recognizing the contributions of each builder type and how each of us inhabits the wolf cycle–as an innocent pig or an ignorant wolf–becomes a grand experience of understanding and insight itself. It is my hope that you will apply the lessons of the wolf cycle to your own experiences, growing in compassion and strengthening your relationships, staying strong in your divine innocence.

CHAPTER 8

THE TRANSFORMATIVE POWER OF DIVINE INNOCENCE

We chose the title of this chapter with you in mind. This title encapsulates the profound theme of this book while conveying both a sense of strength and spiritual growth. The word "transformative" highlights the journey of change and the impact of divine innocence on individuals and society. As you finish reading this book, my hope for you is that you will have the tools you need to live in divine innocence, even in those situations where the wolf is lurking outside the door of your soul. It is this one thing–divine innocence–which will help you express your gifts fully and serve others in such a way that the world is better for you having lived.

The Prevention of Social Cataclysms and Personal Failures

I (Robert) wrote this book with one overarching goal: to save civilization. The ideas presented here are the result of true scientific inquiry—inductive reasoning paired with analytical and synthetic thinking. Now, it is your turn to take the reins. Apply what you've learned. Build upon it through your own observations, reasoning, and analysis. This is how we extend our divine innocence into the realms of knowledge and discovery—by questioning, exploring, and sharing ideas to uncover new horizons of understanding.

Unfortunately, the divine innocence of the scientific method has been obscured by a suffocating pile of preexisting theories. Many of these theories remain unchallenged, stagnating as they collect dust. Instead of questioning them, we've allowed them to become dogma.

"Question everything, even what you've read here."

Yet questioning is the heart of science. It is the lifeblood of discovery. And so I urge you, dear reader: question everything, even what you've read here.

Imagine a single column standing beneath every person. Whether we are straw, stick, or brick builders, this column represents the sum of all our connections—those formed through sensory experiences, memories, emotions, and interactions. But just as the column is built on connections, it is also riddled with disconnections. We forget so many of the good and bad moments that shape us, losing sight of their impact on our lives. Yet the connections that do remain—whether positive or negative—are rooted in our divine innocence.

Every so often, I pause my hectic life to reflect on my first encounters with divine innocence. These moments came through my children. At the time, I did not know I was autistic, nor did I understand the concept of divine innocence. Yet I instinctively responded to their innocence with my own. I wanted to reach deep into their subconscious minds, helping them become their best selves while teaching them to bring out the best in others.

"I pause my hectic life to reflect on my first encounters with divine innocence."

Whenever my children fought, I would remind them: "All the money, success, and fame in the world mean nothing if you spend your lives attacking each other. If you think this fighting will disappear when you're adults, you're wrong. It will carry on." I knew this from personal experience. My brothers had excluded and belittled me as a child, and they still do to this day. This is the nature of wolfish behaviors—they become ingrained in us through practice, shaping who we think we are.

One of my fondest memories with my children is a tradition I (Robert) inherited from my father: tickling feet. Almost every night, as the world quieted and sleep approached, I would gently tickle their feet at bedtime. The touch was soft and soothing, like the cooing of a dove, lulling them into a peaceful slumber. This nightly ritual became a cherished bond between us. Even as teenagers, they would crawl into my bed, asking, "Will you tickle my feet?" Their siblings would follow, lining up for their turn. The youngest would never call out, but they waited patiently, always content to be included.

Sometimes, as I tickled their feet, I would talk to them about God, love, or the unique gifts each of them possessed. Other nights, I read them stories or simply listened as their mother read to them. Later, I learned that the feet are home to thousands of nerve endings, and that a gentle touch stimulates the nervous system in profound ways, much like the music of a Stradivarius violin. I believe this amplified my words, allowing my messages to seep into their subconscious minds.

Looking back, this simple ritual was an expression of my divine innocence—a subconscious, ingenious way to bond with my children and teach them about life. It created a foundation of trust and love that has endured through good times and bad.

While I focused on instilling positivity, I also knew that life is filled with wolves. Giving my children only affirmations and easy experiences would have left them unprepared for the challenges of the real world. I wanted to equip them with the strength and individuality they would need to face adversity. I encouraged their uniqueness, showing them that God's love was their greatest protection.

It would take years for me to fully understand this protective mantle as divine innocence. This inborn gift, activated through our relationship with Christ and expressed through our builder types, is the foundation of who we are. It is our greatest strength against the wolves of the world.

The Gift of God's Voice in Our Divine Innocence

In each of the builder chapters, we explored how each builder type aligns with the Father, Son, and Spirit. We saw how each Person of God gifts the builders with a unique voice, a speaking style that is intrinsic to their personality. In this section, as we prepare to end our time together in this book, we encourage you to pursue observations for builders' voices in your everyday experience. You might begin with this intriguing question: could people's speaking styles reflect something more profound, perhaps even spiritual? As we have seen, the way a person speaks reveals their alignment with one of the Persons of God—Father, Son, or Holy Spirit.

When I (Robert) began my own observations, I saw that the straw builders invariably spoke with a soft and gentle tone, and that this was a reflection of their empathetic connection to the Holy Spirit. After all, the Holy Spirit is often described in Scripture as a still, small voice. From there, I extended this idea to the other builder types. I saw that the stick builder, with their innate desire to save and serve others, is a reflection of Jesus, the Son of God, who came to save humanity? Finally, the brick builder, with their commanding and protective nature, mirrors the voice of God the Father, who delivered the Israelites and established divine law.

This discovery fascinated me, and I have continued to observe how people of different builder types communicate in my social interactions. I listen not just to their words but to their tone, intent, and the underlying energy of their voices.

Straw builders often communicate with a quiet empathy, reflecting the Holy Spirit's role as a gentle guide. Their voice soothes, encourages, and inspires without force, embodying the Spirit's nature as a comforter and counselor. There is a softness in their words, a depth that invites reflection rather than demands attention.

Stick builders, on the other hand, have a natural inclination to see themselves as saviors in their relationships, often stepping in to help, heal, or advocate for others. Their voice carries a tone of personal sacrifice, compassion, and urgency—mirroring Jesus' mission to serve and save humanity. Whether through passionate conviction or unexpected riddles, their speech seeks to challenge and uplift.

Brick builders speak with clarity, authority, and strength. Their tone is commanding but also protective, reflecting the Father's role as a leader and lawgiver. Bricks focus on providing structure and stability, much like the Father's guidance for His people. Their words are direct, unmistakable, and meant to establish order.

Recognizing these distinct voices has given me a deeper appreciation for how each builder type communicates. More importantly, it has helped me approach relationships with greater compassion, understanding that each builder is expressing truth in their own way.

When we all make this effort with one another, we can avoid the wolfish tendency to become frustrated or dismissive when someone's style of communication differs from our own. For example, a brick builder's directness might feel overwhelming to a straw builder, while a straw builder's soft tone might seem ineffective or passive to a brick. Similarly, a stick builder's tendency to act as a savior might be misinterpreted as overbearing. Yet, when we understand these styles as reflections of divine attributes—empathy, service, and authority—we can approach one another with grace and acceptance.

This discovery underscores the idea that each of us has a unique role in expressing God's voice in the world. Whether we are straw, stick, or brick builders, our divine innocence is reflected in the way we communicate, and our voices have the power to uplift, guide, and connect. By embracing and honoring these differences, we not only enhance our relationships but also create a more harmonious and compassionate world.

The Harmony of Divine Innocence

The world cannot function, let alone thrive, on the strength of just one builder type. It requires all three builder types, each with their unique gifts, working together in balance to create a powerhouse of harmonious creativity. This principle holds true for everything from successful businesses to enduring marriages. Nature itself reflects the strength of three. Every carpenter knows that a three-legged stool is inherently more stable than one with four legs, and a stool with only two legs cannot stand at all.

This concept is particularly evident in partnerships. In my work with the wolf cycle, I've observed that when two people of different builder types come together, their partnership benefits most from the presence of someone representing the third type. This third entity doesn't necessarily need to be a person—it can be the divine presence of God, embodying the missing type and completing the triune balance. If both partners share the same builder type, they need two others who embody the missing types to achieve harmony and success. However, this dynamic only works when all individuals are rooted in their divine innocence. Without it, the wolf within can rear its head, undermining collaboration and creating discord.

When harmony is achieved through divine innocence, the results are extraordinary. Partnerships flourish, creativity abounds, and relationships become more resilient. Even in solitary work, we can draw upon others or the divine Persons of God to establish this balance. We have done this many times, and it has profoundly shaped our lives and work.

As the theory of the wolf cycle has matured, it has become increasingly clear to me that this harmony is not just a key to individual and collective success—it is essential for repairing fractured relationships with friends and family. By understanding and embracing the differences between builder types, we can build bridges that foster mutual respect and cooperation.

This harmony is not just practical; it is revolutionary. We believe that when we work in alignment with others through divine innocence, we can save civilization from destruction. This requires intentional effort—learning to love ourselves and others from a place of divine innocence, understanding our builder type, and appreciating the strengths of those who are different from us. When we do this, we create a world where the next generation can thrive.

Our legacy is shaped by the harmony we cultivate today. By living in divine innocence and teaching this principle to our children, we ensure they can carry this torch forward. Our hope is that our children's children will live in even greater alignment with their divine innocence than we have.

Interestingly, the story of the three little pigs itself reflects this progression. You might recall that it began as a whimsical tale about forest pixies in the 17th century, passed down orally by parents to their children. Over generations, it evolved into the written story we know today, and now it takes on an even deeper archetypal meaning as we uncover the profound truths of the pigs' builder types and the divine harmony they represent.

Intuition and the Ethereal

How many people fail in life because they do not listen to their intuition?

Intuition is a gift of our divine innocence. We believe it is the still small voice of the Spirit in our hearts. It is there to guide us. We ignore it at our peril.

Hindsight may be 20/20, but there are times when we have more foresight than we give ourselves credit for.

But there are times when what we think is intuition might not be rooted in our divine innocence but of the world. Then it will lead us astray. I (Robert) remember a story about a woman who was engaged to be married and she wanted to be certain that the marriage was the right thing for her. She went to the Temple to pray and got a message that it wasn't the right thing so she called off the wedding.

Was that 'message' really from her divine innocence? Or was it her own fears and longings that were being vocalized?

So how can we know when intuition is rooted in divine innocence?

For any of us, there are times we 'get a feeling' about whether we should or should not do something. There are stories from the terrorist attack on the World Trade Centers in 2001 that some people had a feeling they should stay home, and they did. Yet one wonders, how many had such a premonition and ignored it?

The sinking of the Titanic is another international disaster where some heeded their intuition and some did not. The parents of Eva Hart, a seven-year-old passenger, are one example. Eva's mother had a strong premonition that they should not board the ship, and she begged her husband to change their plans. She argued that no ship was unsinkable and to persist in such an idea was the height of arrogance. She called it an offense to God. Her husband did not heed her warning. They embarked on the Titanic as planned. When they sailed, Eva's mother stayed up all night as her intuition of disaster persisted. The night of the accident, she was awake when the ship struck the iceberg, and she immediately placed Eva and herself on the lifeboat. Her husband stayed behind with the other men to ensure that women and children were saved first. He did not survive.[2]

This could even apply to the three pigs in the popular version of the story. In the story we remember from childhood, the stick and straw pigs' houses fell because they could not withstand the wolf's attack. We often conclude that their materials were inferior, but perhaps it was their building methods that led to haphazard construction and eventual destruction. As we pondered this, it occurred to me that the pig building with bricks could also have ended up with a poorly constructed home if she had failed to use strong mortar and other proper techniques to keep the brick in place. Perhaps she followed her intuition and reason and used superior building methods. Along this line of reasoning, we wondered if the stick and straw pigs

---

[2] CBC. 1985. "Eva Hart Describes Escaping the Sinking Titanic." https://www.youtube.com/watch?v=TY-28Jn8yxc.

could have had a premonition about their building methods and ignored it.

We believe that experiencing premonitions is a natural and normal part of being human. After all, we are both earthly and divine creatures. Listening to these whispers from the ethereal realm is vital to our survival. It connects us to the Godhead, to our Creator. He has a plan for us. He knows the purpose for our lives, and when we listen to our intuition–whether it comes through as a premonition or as a persistent thought or feeling–we are in the center of His will and in the loving arms of our divine innocence. In this sense, our builder type, as an expression of our divine innocence, frees us from the constraints that most personality types box us into.

In a very real sense, intuition is ethereal. That is, it is a light airy feeling that is otherworldly, even spiritual. We would argue that we all experience it often. It seems to me that the soul responds in a supernatural way to the sensation of touching a dog or a horse or the leaves on a tree. In this sense, touching nature itself in all its grandeur is a way of experiencing the ethereal. Our soul touches the ethereal just as our hands touch these living things. By experiencing these intangibles, we enjoy a deep connection with their sacred presence, their energy and perhaps even their healing powers. Other examples might be cradling a newborn in one's arms or holding the hands of a loved one as they pass. These encounters give us insight into the ethereal nature of divine creation and even into eternity beyond this world.

There is another ethereal moment that we have all had at one time or another. It is the divine and sacred energy that comes from a shocking experience we did not expect. It might be an awakening after a narrowly missed life or death experience, as described above. It might be the sudden passing of a loved one or the equally sudden re-entrance of someone into our lives who we thought was gone forever. Whatever it might be, the idea is that being touched by these ethereal moments alters our lives and the lives around us.

Sometimes the ethereal is a soft whisper. Other times, it is a directional feeling that our intuition is communicating. We often call this a 'gut feeling.' We are meant to act on this feeling. The hairs on the back of our neck should not be ignored as they stand at attention to warn us to avert a disaster or change direction. Often this ethereal experience is a precursor or a warning to be on guard to an impending disorder about to unfold.

It is only after we act on such an ethereal moment that we ultimately avert the unknown. It could simply be an unscheduled delay that prevented a tragedy from taking place. Once we act on that intuition, however, we usually never know what would have happened. We are simply able to go on with our days in peace. Those who ignore that gut feeling meet with the tragedy, and we mourn for them. Often we find that people ascribe reasons to their demise that perhaps miss the real point of their ignored intuition. After all, how could the survivors possibly know that they had failed to pay attention to their intuition?

With this in mind, let us return to the three pigs and their story. Did the straw or stick builders respectively ignore such an ethereal feeling? If so, their fate was sealed by their decision. In addition, history has decided the reason for their fate was their mistaken building materials, but what if it was really their decision to ignore the premonition in their souls? On the other hand, the brick builder was rescued, not through her desire to build out of brick as much, but rather because she listened to her intuition. It was not the brick material, then, that saved her life. It was her willingness to go one step further than her siblings that ultimately saved the entire family from demise.

How to Use the Wolf to Build a Better Home

To remain in the precious space of divine innocence—both within ourselves and in our relationships with others—we must learn to face the wolves that inevitably come to our door. The truth is, no matter how fierce or persistent the wolf may be, we are always capable of withstanding its assaults. When we stand strong in this knowledge, our souls are nourished by the confidence that comes from knowing we can endure. Each time we resist the wolf's destructive forces, we strengthen the walls of our inner home, making it more resilient than ever before.

Yet, this process is not without challenges. At least once in our lives—likely many times—we will find ourselves standing in the rubble of a home blown down by a wolf. This does not mean defeat. Instead, it is an opportunity to rebuild. To do so, we must be willing to feel the pain of what has happened, to sit with the discomfort of our loss, and to resist the temptation to let bitterness take root. Resentment and bitterness are the seeds of ignorance, the tools of the wolf that can lead us to abandon our divine innocence. If they do take root, it is essential to uproot them before they consume our souls and leave us wandering, disconnected from ourselves and others.

Rebuilding our homes in the aftermath of the wolf's destruction requires courage, willpower, and the wisdom of divine innocence. Each time we rebuild, we grow stronger and more confident in our ability to face future challenges. Victory over the wolf is not just about survival—it is about thriving. It is about learning from each encounter, discerning whether the wolf was a predator to be overcome or a teacher to be heeded, and using that understanding to build a better, stronger home.

This process of rebuilding is a deeply teachable moment. It reminds us that even when the wolf blows down our home, it does not destroy us if we remain rooted in innocence. In fact, these moments can breathe new energy into our souls, teaching us to rebuild with greater wisdom and strength. To do this, we must embrace the pain of our losses, touch the rawness of the world's trials, and open our eyes to the unexpected beauty that can emerge from adversity. Forgiving those who have wronged us, releasing resentment, and preventing bitterness from taking root are all essential steps in this process.

When we live from our innocence, we create flourishing, tangible results in our lives. The homes of our souls become sanctuaries— stronger, more resilient, and wiser with each trial we endure. This invigoration of courage and willpower allows us to leave the wolf behind, not with hatred but with gratitude for the lessons learned. In doing so, we accept the wolf's role as a teacher and move forward to live in the peace and harmony of divine innocence.

Breaking the Cycle: A Call to Live in Divine Innocence
We live in a world that is undeniably fallen, where wolves lurk at every turn, and the temptation to succumb to their ways can feel overwhelming. But we do not have to give in. Each of us has the power, through divine innocence, to resist the wolf's wiles and break the cycle of destruction that so often defines human behavior. This book has been an exploration of the ways we can identify, confront, and ultimately transcend the wolf within and around us. Now, as we come to the end, the choice to put these principles into practice is yours.

Being human is a paradoxical experience. We are each unique, unparalleled in our individuality, yet we share so much in common. Our joys and struggles, our loves and losses, all connect us in profound ways. At the heart of this shared experience is a choice: will we build lives of divine innocence, or will we fall prey to the wolf's cycle of ignorance and destruction?

To choose innocence is not to deny the reality of pain, hardship, or even evil. Instead, it is to face these challenges with courage and humility, knowing that we are divinely equipped to overcome them. Part of that divine equipping lies in understanding and embracing our builder types. Whether you are a straw, stick, or brick builder, your unique gifts and strengths are essential to building a better world.

Straw builders, with their quiet wisdom and gentle spirits, bring comfort and clarity to those in turmoil. Their connection to the Holy Spirit enables them to discern truth and offer guidance with empathy and care. Stick builders, bold and courageous, embody the saving spirit of Christ, speaking truth with passion and standing up for those who cannot stand up for themselves. Brick builders, rooted in authority and strength, reflect the Father's steadfast nature, creating order and laying firm foundations for others to build upon. Together, these builder types harmonize to create a balanced and thriving world. Each type brings something invaluable to the table, and when we recognize and honor these differences, we achieve divine harmony and unparalleled creativity.

We cannot rid the world of wolves, but we can refuse to become one ourselves. By choosing to live from divine innocence and aligning with the strengths of our builder type, we weaken the wolf's hold on the world. We break the cycle of hurt begetting hurt, betrayal begetting betrayal, and destruction begetting destruction. Instead, we plant seeds of hope, love, and renewal, nurturing a better future for ourselves and for those who come after us.

As we reflect on the shared experiences of humanity, we are reminded that the most difficult thing we will ever do is something we all must face: death. Yet, we also believe the most beautiful thing we will ever do is something we all have the privilege to share: birth. Both remind us of our sacred connection to the divine and to one another. Our lives, from beginning to end, are expressions of this connection. Every moment, every choice, every interaction is an opportunity to affirm or deny that truth.

So we leave you with this challenge: be vigilant. Build your house strong. Recognize the wolf for what it is, but do not let it define you. When your home is threatened, rebuild it with greater wisdom and strength, drawing on the unique qualities of your builder type to guide you. Teach these principles to your children, your friends, your neighbors. Pass on the legacy of divine innocence so that they, too, can withstand the storms of life and resist the wolf's call.

We cannot escape living in a world of wolves, but we can choose to rise above them. In doing so, we not only transform our own lives but also contribute to the greater good of humanity. Together, with the harmony of the straw, stick, and brick builders, we can break the cycle and build a better world—one home, one heart, one soul at a time.

REVIEWS

Prior to reading this book, I was not well-versed in personality types, nor had I understood fully how my personality type affects (or can affect) my true nature either in positive or negative ways. For this reason, I found *The Wolf Cycle* compelling, as it explained personality types in a way that were understandable and effective for me.

Most everyone has heard or read the story of the three little pigs and the big bad wolf. Mr. Bautner (Robert) uses this story at the beginning of this book and then expounds on it throughout to simply and effectively explain three specific personality types. Then developing on these types, he explains further how each one of us might think or act in good or bad ways, depending on our own specific personality type, where bad refers to the "wolf" that can present itself in us if we allow it. Finally, he provides insights and examples of how we are capable of avoiding or moving away from the "wolf" in ourselves and returning to our true nature, which he refers to as our "divine innocence." As we do so, we effectively build a better house (a better life) for ourselves. Robert also draws frequently from his own experiences in life, giving this book a personal touch that is sometimes missing in other treatises.

If you are like me and want to better understand who you are and want to avoid and/or eliminate the "wolfish" tendencies in your life then this book can provide you answers that you may not have considered previously. Thank you, Robert!

Stan S., Salt Lake City, UT

My name is Bampoe Abraham from Ghana. I have been fortunate enough to read *The Wolf Cycle* which is one of the best books I have read. It is very relatable to my life experience and I would like to share a few of my thoughts with you.

I have come to understand that each of us—no matter who we are, where we come from, or what we do—will face challenges in life. Whether or not we remain connected to our divine innocence, we are vulnerable to attacks from wolfish personalities, as illustrated in the story of the three little pigs. Yet all we have to do is return to our divine innocence, and it will teach us the correct principles and truths in life. It is this innocence that empowers us to overcome life's challenges. This is the assurance that Robert shares with us.

Another thought is that, regardless of the information we receive from family, friends, or our environment—whether it shapes us positively or negatively—we must remain humble enough to allow God's influence in our lives. This humility enables us to relinquish the wolf within our souls and embrace divine truth, refining us into the best version of who God intends us to be.

My final thought is we all fall into the category of personalities mentioned which is the straw, stick and brick. We need to know who we are, figure out our strengths and weaknesses, and seek to work on ourselves. This will enable us to build a well-structured and strong house so that the wolves, both in the world and in us, will not eat us up and destroy us.

Bampoe A., Ghana

We all know the story of the three pigs and the wolf. If you are like me, you always thought the moral of the story was to build the strongest house, the brick house of course so it would withstand the wolf. In this wonderful and surprising spin to the story we get a closer, more personal look at each of the pigs and the wolf, and we come to realize that the straw and stick houses could be as strong as the brick house.

By looking at the personalities of the characters in this famous fable we can easily see ourselves and others and what house they would build. What is most interesting is that each of the pigs and the wolf, yes even the wolf, have qualities that are desirable, and that each of us can fall prey to the wolf inside of us. The examples that are given are very vivid and help the reader to really see inside each of the characters and view the world through their eyes. I truly enjoyed reading and then rereading this book to try to understand which pig I really am, and I know you will enjoy it as well.

Adam W., Salt Lake City, UT

BAUTNER & HELMLING

ABOUT ROBERT BAUTNER

 Robert is an author, businessman, and father of five. When he is not writing, he is caring for his clients' horses on his property in a beautiful mountain valley of Utah. He encourages people to look at life through a new lens, particularly people who are struggling with differentness. His life's work is turning negatives into positives and viewing it all as a journey of authenticity and grace.

If anyone had told him when he was a young man that he would become an author, he would have told them they were crazy. Growing up in an abusive household, Robert was led to believe that he was mentally retarded because of his unusual thinking patterns and speech. That was added to his dyslexia, which made reading difficult. Too many times to count, his mother said, "You talk in riddles! Can't you talk intelligent?"

He spent the majority of his life uncomfortable with himself, masking his undiagnosed autism by mimicking and copying others. He studied people's behaviors intently, including facial expressions, physical stance, tone, word usage, and even looks. The first step away from this inauthentic life was his autism diagnosis at age 55. He began a journey of self-discovery that is ongoing. The more he learned about autism, the more he became aware that his way of being was not unintelligent at all. He never stopped speaking in riddles, but he did realize that a mind filled with riddles is an untapped treasure.

Although he spent half his life avoiding his true nature, he deeply values those years. They led him to seek and recognize patterns in human behavior in far more detail than he otherwise would have. They also guided him to focus intently on the nature of God and people's divine connections with Him–Father, Son, and Holy Spirit. When these elements were combined with his autistic way of looking at the world, a new vision, a new perspective, even an expanded way of living in divine innocence, was born. As he sees it, our divine innocence unites us with God in His holy innocence, and it is from this relationship that our success in life is born.

His dream is to share this perspective with his readers. His first book, *Stop Your Crying*, is a powerful and poignant story of how one autistic boy overcame the trauma of abuse and achieved all his dreams. This book, *The Wolf Cycle*, is his second. He has also co-authored three books in the bestselling series called *Human Empowerment*. He is currently writing his third book, *One Reason to Stay*. Learn more at *https://robertbautner.com*.

ABOUT LARA HELMLING

Lara Helmling is a publisher, editor, author, and advocate for authors. She founded Forest City Publications, where she assists writers and entrepreneurs in enhancing their writing skills and empowering them to publish professionally and independently. Lara's academic background weaves together literature, psychology, and the study of science in society, giving her a unique interdisciplinary lens on human behavior, storytelling, and cultural evolution. She also spent twelve years early in her career teaching elementary and middle school, where she learned the beauty and importance of the perspectives of people with special needs.

In addition, Lara Helmling is the founder and creative force behind Tickled Pink Flamingos, an off-grid vintage camper campground and retreat center located in the Petrified Forest in Arizona. She is developing the property into a unique destination for creatives, nature lovers, and wellness seekers looking to unplug from modern life while still enjoying intentional comforts. Her vision blends eco-conscious living with creative entrepreneurship to build a legacy that celebrates both innovation and simplicity.

She splits her time between family in Ames, Iowa and the high desert of the Petrified Forest, Arizona. She enjoys reading, crafting, painting, walks with her dog Sam, and watching Sam and her calico Caiomhe play. Learn more about Lara's work at: https://tickledpinkflamingos.com and https://forestcitypublications.com.

FOR YOUR NEXT READ

HOW ONE AUTISTIC BOY SAVED
HIS WORLD

"I wish I never had you."
My mother said these words to me
more times than I can count.
I grew up in a household of wolves,
protected by the unshakable divine
innocence of my autism.
This is my story.
ROBERT BAUTNER

AVAILABLE AT ALL MAJOR
BOOKSELLERS

FOR YOUR NEXT READ

Raised in an abusive, anti-Mormon environment, Author Robert Bautner learned to turn negatives into positives in order to survive. But it wasn't until he came to faith in Jesus and became a member of the Church of Jesus Christ of Latter-day Saints that he began to thrive. He married, fathered five children, was wrongly diagnosed with schizophrenia, then rightly diagnosed with autism, and finally divorced against his wishes. Through it all he witnessed 101 reasons to leave, but always found the ONE reason to stay.

COMING OUT 2026

FOR YOUR NEXT READ

Author Robert Bautner joins an extraordinary lineup of thought leaders and celebrity experts—including Erik Swanson, Brian Tracy, Sharon Lechter, Dr. Tony Alessandra—in this bestselling book series focused on unlocking your fullest potential. Through powerful stories, lived experiences, and practical insights, Robert shares how trust and integrity shaped his personal transformation. His voice stands out among 33+ inspiring co-authors who teach how to build a life of purpose, align with community, and rise through empowered action.

Now Available on Amazon, Barnes & Noble, and all major booksellers. Learn more at:

www.TheBookOfHumanEmpowerment.com